Professional Programming Tools for C and C++

1

Professional Programming Tools for C and C++

Anton Gerdelan
Illustrated by Katja Žibrek

Professional Programming Tools for C and C++

ISBN: 978-1-5272-5848-8

First printing

Published by Anton Gerdelan and Katja Žibrek
antongerdelan.net

About the cover: The cover image was the result of a short discussion between the authors. *"Most programming books have a picture of mountains or animals. We should just do a cartoon of ourselves, or a startled beaver."*

Contents

Preface

About this Book

This book presents a quick start to a full range of tools you can use for programming and shipping quality software written in the C or C++ programming languages. Each chapter addresses an important program development task, and introduces tools for completing the task on all the major desktop operating systems. We try to minimise the discussion, and get you started right away with practical instructions, adding hints and tips for common issues at the end of each chapter.

Programming books are mostly written as entry-level introduction to topics or at a very advanced level, and there isn't much bridging material available for those in the years in-between. When we started writing this book we were thinking of coders in the experience ranges between doing a degree and more specialised career roles. In particular, coders wanting to get into work in the industry, but unsure if they are missing some skills, tools, and techniques that weren't part of an academic education or learned for research projects. This book's reviewers have been programming for many years, and they also picked up some useful new tools and techniques from reading this text, so there may well be something new here for more experienced programmers too.

C and C++ programming languages are very powerful, but have some memory and security vulnerabilities that require special attention. This book will get the reader up to speed with standard programming tools used with many languages, but also with specialist tools like fuzzers and static code analysers that are particularly useful for finding flaws in C and C++ programs.

Rest assured that you may use many of the same techniques from this book in other programming languages, including web technology, with some slightly different tools and functions. In any case it is beneficial for all programmers to spend some time with C, reasoning about memory allocation and memory access patterns. These are important skills with respect to performance for modern computers in any programming language, but can be abstracted further from the sight of the programmer in other languages.

In my previous book project, *Anton's OpenGL 4 Tutorials*, people really liked my hand-drawn diagrams, but I'm not a very talented artist! I teamed up with my friend Dr Katja Žibrek who illustrated this book. I'm really happy with how much clearer, and funnier, the diagrams are now! We hope that programmers in graphics and games, computer vision, compilers and operating systems, embedded systems, simulations, machine learning, and many other areas, pick up some useful tools and techniques from the short articles in this book. We also hope you find it fun.

The last content chapter, *"Argh! My New Job is on Linux! - Unix Tools"*, is not specific to C or C++ but is an increasingly common scenario for coders in a modern office. C is the language of Unix, and Unix derived-systems have always supported C and C++ development. C++ is very popular in the 3D graphics world, where coders have mostly been based on Windows. These days we're seeing a lot of graphics on embedded devices and AR/VR headsets, which often run on a little Linux device. We also see teams commonly using a variety of virtualised or Docker-container Linux systems to distribute code or run servers. It felt right to include a chapter on Unix tools here, with a focus on monitoring and getting the most out of your C programs.

We challenged ourselves to keep this book short, so had to leave a lot of useful topics out. In particular, it would be really valuable for those entering industry roles to follow a "day in the life" view of how a programmer in industry works in a team, their collaboration tools and processes, version control tools such as Git, reporting tools, and how we are expected to work with designers, QA, and product teams in a modern office. Look out for future volumes!

This book is self-published and designed to be affordable for students, so there will be some rough edges that you wouldn't normally expect. We think that this is a good compromise for most readers, but it's not everyone's favourite. Hopefully you can also pick up some of our enthusiasm for doing good work in the area, and make learning and teaching a top career priority. For errata and further information see http://antongerdelan.net/pro_programming_tools_book/.

Assumed Knowledge

The basics of programming with C and C++ are not covered in this book. You should already be able to write at least a few simple C programs with loops, arrays, `printf()` and text file output, and know the basics of dynamic memory allocation. You should know that

```
int* my_pointer = malloc( 16 * sizeof( int ) );
```

allocates heap memory large enough to store 16 integers, and stores the address of the first byte of that in `my_pointer`.

The compiler is the most useful C programming tool of course, but I expect you already know how to compile and link a simple program with your chosen compiler, e.g.

```
gcc main.c
```

Even if you're using a different compiler with different settings and flags, it's a helpful competency to also know the basics of GCC or Clang. GCC and Clang are used everywhere in the industry and almost everywhere to compile free and open source software; which is in turn used by non-free industry software extensively. You will certainly need to compile some of it in your career.

If you're not comfortable with these topics yet then I suggest the following might be a useful start:

- Find instructions for installing a C compiler for your operating system.
- Buy or borrow an entry-level C programming book.
- Take a short course or follow video tutorials (the first results I looked through on YouTube were all pretty good).
- Follow some online tutorials such as those at https://www.cprogramming.com/, which will get you up to speed for free.
- Ask for advice, code reviews, or mentoring from experienced C programmers.

The good news is that C is quite a small language that doesn't take long to learn. If you're coming from another programming language this should be quite do-able.

Code Examples

Rest assured that the tools described in this book apply equally well to C and C++. To keep example snippets fairly generic to versions of both languages the code examples in this book are written in C99, without relying on any features that diverge from C++. This should compile as C or C++ on most compilers without any special compiler flags, and without any major code changes.

If you need to use C89 you probably already know how to change the single line comments and declare-anywhere variables to suit your compiler. C++ users may wish to explicitly cast the type of the pointer returned by `malloc()`, or may prefer to use **new** instead.

```
/* C89 */
int* my_pointer = malloc( 16 * sizeof( int ) );


// C++ with a C-style cast. `static_cast` may also be used.
int* my_pointer = (int*)malloc( 16 * sizeof( int ) );
// C++ with `new` instead of malloc().
int* my_pointer = new int [16];
```

Avoid copy-pasting code from book examples when you're learning - you are much better served rewriting it all yourself in your own style. To see how each snippet may fit into a small, complete, program, there is a repository of code examples at https://github.com/capnramses/pro_programming_tools_c_cpp.

Reading Recommendations

If you like short, useful, programming books similar to this, but with a creative task:

- *Ray Tracing in One Weekend* (Ray Tracing Minibooks Book 1), by Peter Shirley. Digital. 2016.
- *Make Your Own Neural Network*, by Tariq Rashid. CreateSpace, 2016. ISBN-13: 978-1530826605

I think my strongest recommendation has to be Peter Shirley's *Ray Tracing In One Weekend* series of mini-books. Ray tracing is a method for creating 3D graphics. The books are easy to get into - you can write your own 3D graphics-creating ray tracer program with the exact tools and technologies described in this book - no fancy graphics cards or libraries are required.

If you're interested in the Deep Learning boom *Make Your Own Neural Network* is a pretty easy practical how-to guide to writing a handwriting recognition program. It's Python-based, but I was able to pretty easily write a C version based on the Python examples, which is on my GitHub https://github.com/capnramses/neural_net_handwriting.

For C Programming:

- *The C Programming Language*, 2nd Edition, by Brian W. Kernighan and Dennis M. Ritchie. Prentice-Hall, 1978. ISBN: 0131103628.
- *Expert C Programming: Deep Secrets*, by Peter van der Linden. Prentice Hall, 1994. ISBN-13: 978-0131774292.
- https://en.wikipedia.org/wiki/C99

These books are quite old now. I mostly use C99, which has a few convenience features over the venerable C89 (*AKA* C90). C11 is also used, but not quite as widely supported across compilers. I suggest supplementing the above books with some quick reading over the new features in C99 and C11. Thankfully C is pretty small so that's only a few minutes of reading!

1 Coding Assertively with Assertions

Assertions are a basic run-time test for program state correctness, and can save you a lot of time. If given an expression that resolves to false, an assertion prints the file name and line number of the failing call, and raises SIGABRT.This deliberately crashes the program in C, but it can also be intercepted by a **debugger** to help analyse the cause of failure. If the expression resolves to true then it does nothing.

{ Assertions }

```
int counter = 100;
assert (counter < 100);

bool return_success = some_function();
assert (return_success);
```

it will resolve to false and fail

I'm true!

Nope! Bye bye

Google Test

→ most **unit testing** frameworks provide non-crashing checks or assertions as their core functions, also collect statistics

type (man 3 assert) to retrieve manual for C assertions

Why Use Assertions

- Test your logical assumptions when writing code, and catch incorrect or unexpected state.
- In-code assertions are very time-effective and flexible to write during coding.
- If the program crashes it forces you to get the problem fixed right away. Fixing bugs before writing more code is always a good habit for quality of work.
- Continuing a program with out-of-control state can lead to very complex bugs later in execution, that take longer to diagnose.
- They are especially helpful when learning, for testing your assumptions about how things actually work, getting each concept right before moving on.
- Can be removed from release builds. In C or C++ define NDEBUG to remove all the assertions from a build.
- Can catch unexpected changes elsewhere in the code that break your code at a later time.
- When used aggressively, can be used as an alternative technique to formal test programs and test-driven development (TDD). This can be very handy for tests in code that is iterated on and changes frequently, where updating formal test frameworks would slow you down.

How and When to Use Assertions

1. Include `<assert.h>`
2. Call `assert( your_boolean_variable_or_expression_here );`
3. Run your program, and check the printed output for abort reports.
4. Use a debugger to trace the stack of function calls and parameter values that lead up to the assertion failing.

A good strategy is to test the inputs of each function for validity, e.g. NULL pointers, or check if values used to index arrays will be within bounds. As a rule of thumb, any code where you think...

"Argh! If this variable is ever negative / NULL / too large / false, the code will break!"

...then it is a good place to guard with an assertion. The assertion might pass for now, but if you leave it in, the assertion can catch a breaking change to the code at a later date.

Assertions are not appropriate when your program should gracefully handle an issue and continue running. This usually includes attempting to load a file, or occasions where reporting an error to the user is more appropriate.

```c
#include <string.h>
#include <stdio.h>
#include <assert.h>

/*
Change a character in a string to the null terminator.
Asserts if out of bounds.
PARAMS
str       - A char array. Cannot be a NULL pointer.
str_len   - Maximum bytes allocated for length of str.
str_index - Byte index in str to change to `\0`.
*/
void my_str_truncate( char* str, int str_len, int str_index ) {
  // Abort program if str was NULL.
  assert( str );
  // Abort if str_index was outside of allowed range
  assert( str_index >= 0 && str_index < str_len );

  str[str_index] = '\0';
}

int main() {
  char name[10];
  strncpy( name, "anton", 10 );
  int new_length = 3; // try changing to a number >= 10
  my_str_truncate( name, 10, new_length );
  // should print "ant"
  printf( "truncated: %s\n", name );

  return 0;
}
```

Unit Testing and Assertions

You may also use assertions to **unit test** for correct outputs of your functions in a test program. A unit test typically checks a set of inputs for a unit of code versus known correct outputs. Our "unit" is a function here.

```c
#include <assert.h>

/* trivial function to add two integers */
int my_adder( int a, int b ) {
  return a + b;
}

void run_tests() {
  int a_inputs[3]        = { 0,   100, -100 };
  int b_inputs[3]        = { 0, -200,  200 };
  int expected_outputs[3] = { 0, -100,  100 };
  for ( int i = 0; i < 3; i++ ) {
    int result = my_adder( a_inputs[i], b_inputs[i] );
    assert( expected_outputs[i] == result );
  }
}
```

To have a unit testing assertion that collects statistics and write reports out on tests passed without stopping the program, you could write your own macro, or you can use a unit testing framework:

- Check for C https://libcheck.github.io/check/.
- Google Test for C++ https://github.com/google/googletest.

Test frameworks require additional boiler-plate code, and so require a bit more time investment. Usually similar tests need to be grouped into *suites*, using some macros in your test program. These tools can be integrated as part of an automated build process for release builds.

Tips and Common Problems

For best effect assertions should be used in combination with other testing and debugging tools. When combined with an interactive debugger, a back-trace of functions called, and logging and printing of errors and warnings, a programmer can very rapidly diagnose, follow, and reason about problems in even very complex code with many people contributing to it.

- For small projects assertions may be all you need, but for production code, assertions should not be your only code tests. It is common to see studios pair heavy use of in-code assertions with an automated *"smoke & build"* test, or automated **fuzz testing**.
- When an assertion fails it also prints the expression that failed. You can exploit this to add a string of text to the output.

```
assert( name != NULL && "name parameter was NULL" );
```

- You can define NDEBUG when compiling to remove all the assert calls from a build, e.g.

```
gcc -DNDEBUG main.c
```

- Don't call any functions, or put any code that changes program state, inside the assertion: e.g. assert(render()). Release builds often define NDEBUG, which will remove the assertion macros, including any code called inside assert() parentheses!
- Code inside an assert expression can also cause a **Heisenbug** - a bug that goes away when you run a debugger to find it - when NDEBUG is not set.
- If you want a special assert() that also works reliably in release builds you can create your own macro that tests an input and calls abort().
- I have even heard of studios that leave assertions in shipped code, to force

bugs to be found and fixed immediately, and not allow an app to get into an unstable state.

- A custom `assert()` can be used to programmatically trigger debugger breakpoints to help you analyse the failing condition in a debugger. The method for doing this varies per debugger and platform.
- A custom `assert()` macro can also print or log more detailed information, such as a **backtrace** of function calls to help you diagnose and reproduce a reported crash very quickly.
- Many IDEs (Integrated Development Environment) will recognise the printed output of `assert()` and let you click on it to jump to the file and line.
- Most fuzz testing tools will count assertions as crashes to fix. In this case you need to gracefully handle any invalid inputs without crashing.
- **CMake** builds can quietly enable `NDEBUG` on release builds without you asking for it. If your assertions aren't working, maybe that's why.
- Some languages have a "static" version of assertions for compile-time checks. C11 and C++11 have `static_assert()`. These assertions are useful for ensuring the size of different types or the values of enumerated types.

2 Writing Out an Image File

Why Image Output is Useful

- It's fun to get some visual output.
- For people learning it's a great feedback buzz after dry, console-printing exercises.
- Visually debugging problems by writing data to an image, especially geometric or graphical data, is really handy.
- You can dump a quick chart or visualisation of any data you are working with.
- It's easy to do.

Working with Image Memory

1. Determine image dimensions and channel count.
2. Dynamically allocate memory. Don't use fixed-length arrays on the stack - images can easily require more than the available stack memory.
3. Understand contiguous pixel memory and how to index it.
4. Write into image memory's colour channels for a pixel.

We typically work with images held in blocks of bytes in main memory. Think of an array. Each pixel, if a coloured image, is typically represented by 3 bytes - a first byte representing the red colour contribution, a second byte representing the green colour contribution, and a third byte representing the blue colour contribution. This is called **RGB** (red-green-blue) format, and we can say that it has 3 **colour channels**. If each colour channel has 1 byte then there are 256 possible shades (values 0 to 255) of each, giving a combined 24-bits per pixel colour description. There are many other colour arrangements. **Greyscale** may have 1 channel and 1 byte. There may be an additional **alpha** channel, representing opacity, or some other special property of the image. **BGR** images have the same 3 channels but in reverse order.

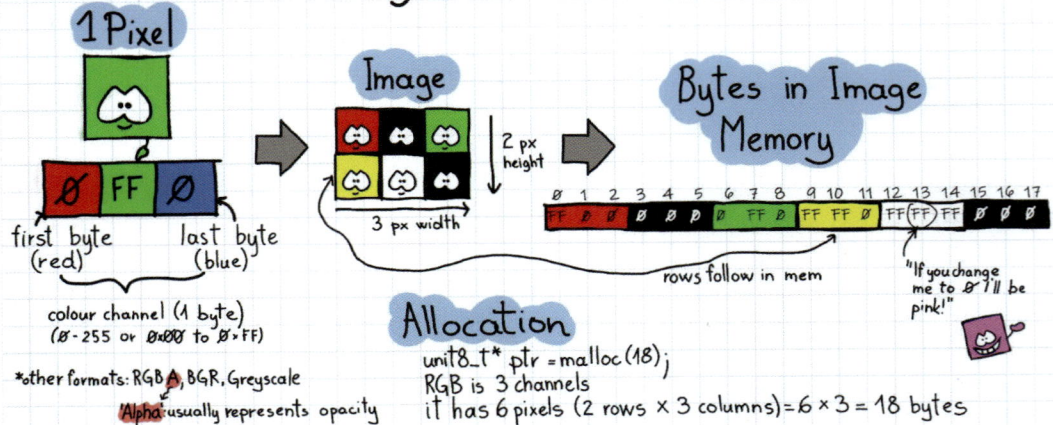

Figure 2.1. The 6 RGB pixels in this image require 18 bytes of memory - 3 bytes per pixel.

Given the number of channels n_channels, and the width and height of the image we want to work with, we can allocate memory for it. To represent 1 byte in C you can use **unsigned char**, or **uint8_t** if you #include <stdint.h>.

```
uint8_t* image_ptr = malloc( width * height * n_channels );
```

You can alternatively use calloc(), which also initialises all the memory allocated to zero. That's handy for images because it sets your initial colour to black.

Images start counting their pixels usually in either the top-left or bottom-left corner, and if you follow the memory order, you will write the 3 colour bytes for the first pixel, then the 3 colour bytes for the pixel to the right, and so on, until the end of the row. Then starting again at the left-hand side of the next row. This is essentially one long 1D array.

To retrieve the index of a particular pixel in our image memory, given by an (x,y) coordinate in the image, we can get an index into the memory with:

```
int pixel_idx = n_channels * ( y * width + x );
```

For an RGB image this gives us the index of that pixel's red channel. To get the green channel byte's index add +1, and +2 for blue.

To set the colour of a pixel:

```
image_ptr[ pixel_idx + 0 ] = 0xFF; // red channel
image_ptr[ pixel_idx + 1 ] = 0x00; // green channel
image_ptr[ pixel_idx + 2 ] = 0x7F; // blue channel
```

I've used hexadecimal numbers here for convenience, but you can also use the decimal numbers. Just remember that each channel is only one byte, so only decimal values 0-255 (00-FF in hexadecimal) are valid. You may have just had an *"Aha!"* moment thinking about how HTML colours are expressed?

With this knowledge we can draw into the image we keep in memory, at any pixel we wish. You might find it convenient to write a function similar to:

```
draw_pixel( uint8_t* image_ptr, int x, int y, uint8_t r, uint8_t g, uint8_t b )
```

Or you can loop over image memory to fill regions

```
// paint half of the image
for ( int y = 0; y < height; y++ ) {
    for ( int x = 0; x < width / 2; x++ ) {
        int pixel_idx = n_channels * ( y * width + x );
        image_ptr[pixel_idx + 0] = 255; // red channel
        image_ptr[pixel_idx + 2] = 255; // blue channel
    }
}
```

Output a File

- We can dump the image memory out "as is" as a raw image file. But viewing software doesn't know the dimensions or channel count.
- We can use a simple, well-known file format to add this information ahead of the data. PPM ("Portable Pixel Map") is one of the simplest that is supported by viewers.

Let's use PPM. It has a typical structure of a **header** containing the file type and dimensions and then a **body** containing the image data. The header is in ASCII (American Standard Code for Information Interchange) text. That means when we write P6 at the top it's 2 bytes. The ASCII code for 'P', and then the ASCII code for '6'. Not the value 6! This is a convention with binary files, 2 or 3 ASCII code bytes at the start to indicate what type of file it is.

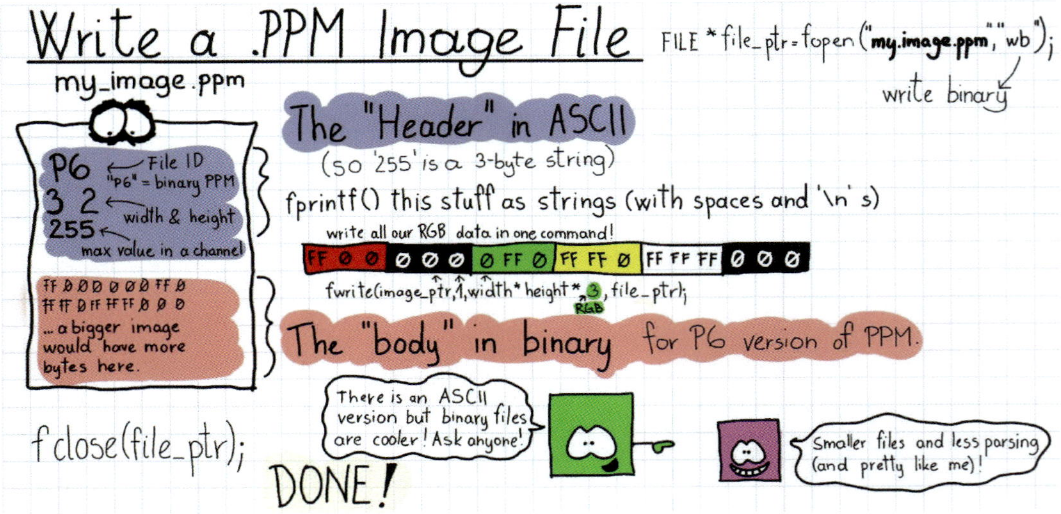

Figure 2.2. The PPM P6 format has an ASCII header (strings) and a binary body (our image data array).

I start by finding the file format specifications online. Wikipedia sometimes documents these quite well. Our image is 3-channel RGB, which you can see in the specification is the case for P3 (ASCII) and P6 (binary) types, with file extension .ppm. Let's use the binary format - P6. Our image data is already binary, we just need to plop that directly into a file for PPM.

Image Output Full Program Listing

```c
#include <stdio.h>
#include <stdint.h>
#include <stdlib.h>

int main() {
  int width = 256, height = 128, n_channels = 3;
  // allocate memory. calloc() sets all our memory to zero (black)
  uint8_t* image_ptr = calloc( 1, width * height * n_channels );

  // paint half the image image (or edit whatever you like here)
  for ( int y = 0; y < height; y++ ) {
    for ( int x = 0; x < width / 2; x++ ) {
      int pixel_idx = n_channels * ( y * width + x );
      image_ptr[pixel_idx + 0] = 255;     // red
      image_ptr[pixel_idx + 2] = 255; // blue
    }
  }
  { // write file
    FILE* fptr = fopen( "out.ppm", "wb" );

    // write header (ASCII)
    fprintf( fptr, "P6\n" );
    fprintf( fptr, "%i %i\n", width, height );
    fprintf( fptr, "255\n" );

    // write body (binary RGB image data)
    fwrite( image_ptr, 1, width * height * n_channels, fptr );

    fclose( fptr );
  }
  free( image_ptr );
  return 0;
}
```

Drawing Lines, Shapes, Gradients, and GIFs

If you have a `draw_pixel()` function, you can supplement this with `draw_line()`, `fill_area()` and so on, to give yourself some tools to output simple charts and visualisations.This will enable you to quickly plot a series of data points to visualise your algorithm's progress, helping to debug or understand it with ease. For line drawing you can implement Bresenham's line algorithm in a function. To make this look nicer you could upgrade to Xiaolin Wu's line algorithm, which adds anti-aliasing so it looks less pixelated. Wikipedia has excellent descriptions of both of these algorithms.

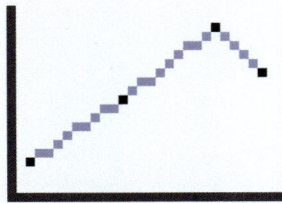

Figure 2.3. We can add a few functions to create quick visualisations or chart data outputs.

To draw gradients or other interesting patterns you can use linear interpolation (*lerp*) or sine wave functions, using the coordinates of each pixel as inputs. To generate a rainbow of colours I used a `lerp()` function where the red value of each pixel was `0xFF` at x `==` 0, down to 0 at x `>` width `/` 2. Green ramped up to the middle of the image, then down again, and blue was zero if x `<` width `/` 2, and after that ramped up to `0xFF` at x `==` width.

Figure 2.4. A higher resolution output, generated by the same PPM-writing C program.

If you have a series of images, such as the steps in a sorting algorithm, and you number the filenames, then you can combine them into an animated GIF file or video using GIMP or ffmpeg.

Other Image Formats

- TGA (Truevision Graphics Adapter) format is only slightly more complex - it supports alpha channel and more image viewers can open it.
- Some bitmap formats have trickier memory layouts and headers - Microsoft BMP (bitmap) is a somewhat more sophisticated binary image file format.
- Some formats such as PNG (Portable Network Graphics) or JPEG (Joint Photographic Experts Group) compress the data to keep file size down, but you need to encode/decode image memory when writing/reading.
- Many formats are binary, but some allow you to save an image in ASCII text, which lets you debug it in a text editor.
- If you want to upgrade to supporting more file format outputs, let me suggest the excellent single-file drop-in library `stb_image_write.h` https://github.com/nothings/stb.

Tips and Common Problems

- If you can't open a PPM file with your default system image viewer, open it with GIMP or IrfanView.
- *"But how do I debug a binary file? We should have just used the ASCII version!"*. And now I reveal the genius of my plan! This was a lead-in to talking about another great debugging (and hacking) tool in the following chapter - **hex editors**!
- Test your image code on tiny 2x2 or so images first - it's much easier to reason about, and debug, small problem domains. Scale up later.
- Many image viewers will upscale or zoom small images for viewing with added **anti-aliasing** effects, which can make your pixel-exact images look blurry. If in doubt, open in an image editor such as GIMP.
- When finding the index of a pixel in memory, it's easy to forget to multiply by the number of channels, and modify the wrong byte.
- It's also easy to forget the number of channels when modifying and make a similar mistake, or extend outside of your memory bounds. I use the n_channels as a variable, rather than hard-coded numbers, wherever I can to mitigate this mistake.
- When working with memory and pointers you may get some interesting run-time errors and memory segmentation violations - the program can throw `SIGSEGV` and crash. It's a good idea when testing to deliberately make mistakes with memory bounds to see what happens (and find out what will work without warning you), even when it's incorrect and unstable.
- Always initialise all your variables to something. I used `calloc()` instead of `malloc()`, to explicitly zero-out my allocated image memory. If you forget to do this it may just so happen to be zero when testing and *work on your machine*, but will break as soon as your friend tries running it. In our case this might mean that unexpected colours will be written into the image where we didn't explicitly set any pixel colours.

- It's easy to mix up ASCII character codes representing numbers, and the numerical values those characters display. You'll run into this when storing the width and height values in your file. These are stored in ASCII in PPM, even in the binary version of the format, which is unusual. 42 in ASCII is represented by two bytes - the byte for the character 4, and the byte for the character 2. The value 42 itself, however, only requires 1 byte to store in a binary file.
- If you write out a numbered sequence of images, at each iteration of your simulation, for example, then you can easily compose them into an animated GIF (Graphics Interchange Format) or movie file. This is a great way to visualise your program, debug it, and demonstrate it.

3 Binary Files and Hex Editors

If you've just written a PPM image out in binary format, then a **hex editor** is your text editor equivalent for inspecting the content of the binary file. You can find problems writing files, or inspect a new type of file to figure out its structure for reading it.

Why use Binary Files

Binary files have a few advantages compared to text files.

- More straightforward file-to-memory and memory-to-file relationships in most cases (less parsing).
- More space-efficient and precise encoding of numbers.
- Lots of file formats are binary, and not that hard to read and write without using a library.
- Some very useful binary file formats conventions exist, derived from the IFF (Interchange File Format) family (WAV audio, BMP images, AIFF audio etc). If you learn how to work with them efficiently they can be a very useful alternative to consider alongside JSON (JavaScript Object Notation) and XML (Extensible Markup Language) for your project's custom files.

As an example, storing the integer 1048576 in ASCII requires 8 bytes - one byte for the ASCII code of each character, plus one byte at the end for the space to separate it. Storing the number in binary, however, can be done with the 4-byte value of the original integer.

Representing floating point values in ASCII files is generally not a good idea because it also introduces issues with preserving precision.

Why use a Hex Editor

Hex editors are particularly useful when writing a program to read a binary file into the program's memory. You can inspect the byte values in the file, and compare that to your assumptions about the data layout.

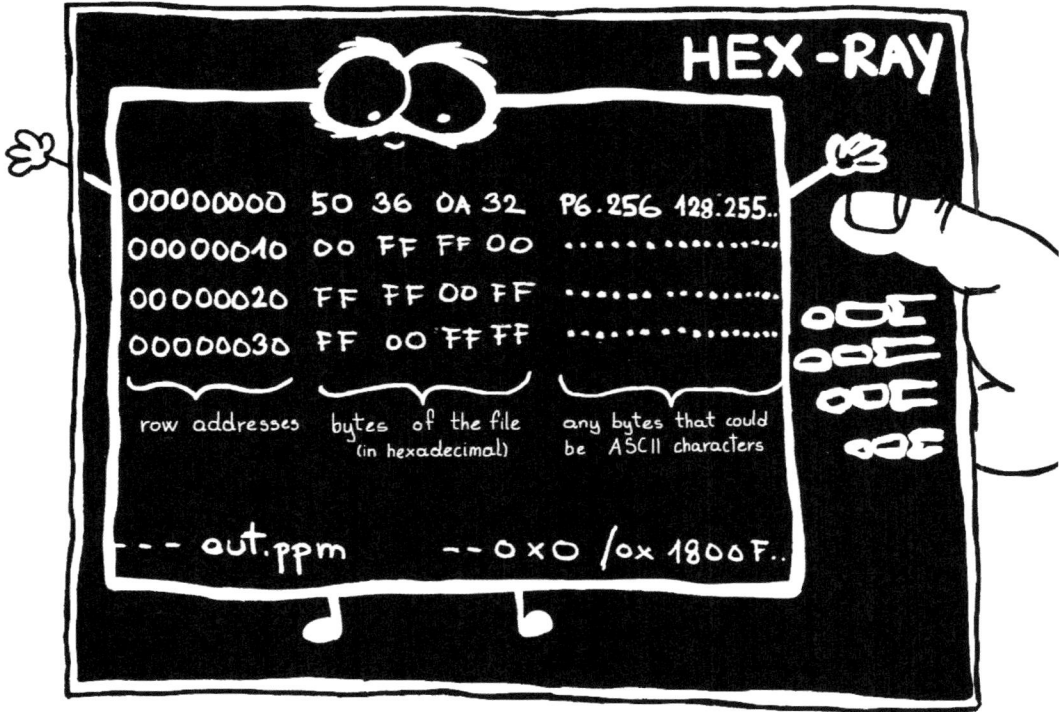

A PPM File in hexedit

HEX -RAY

00000000	50 36 0A 32	P6.256 128.255..
00000010	00 FF FF 00	....
00000020	FF FF 00 FF	....
00000030	FF 00 FF FF	....

row addresses | bytes of the file (in hexadecimal) | any bytes that could be ASCII characters

--- out.ppm   -- 0x0 /0x 1800F..

```
┌─ ▪ Terminal - anton@the_technodrome: ~/projects/antons_howto_guides/02_im  ⇧ _ ▢ ✕
│  File   Edit   View   Terminal   Tabs   Help
│00000000  50 36 0A 32  35 36 20 31  32 38 0A 32  35 35 0A FF   P6.256 128.255..
│00000010  00 FF FF 00  FF FF 00 FF  FF 00 FF FF  00 FF FF 00   ..............
│00000020  FF FF 00 FF  FF 00 FF FF  00 FF FF 00  FF FF 00 FF   ..............
│00000030  FF 00 FF FF  00 FF FF 00  FF FF 00 FF  FF 00 FF FF   ..............
│00000040  00 FF FF 00  FF FF 00 FF  FF 00 FF FF  00 FF FF 00   ..............
│00000050  FF FF 00 FF  FF 00 FF FF  00 FF FF 00  FF FF 00 FF   ..............
│00000060  FF 00 FF FF  00 FF FF 00  FF FF 00 FF  FF 00 FF FF   ..............
│00000070  00 FF FF 00  FF FF 00 FF  FF 00 FF FF  00 FF FF 00   ..............
│00000080  FF FF 00 FF  FF 00 FF FF  00 FF FF 00  FF FF 00 FF   ..............
│00000090  FF 00 FF FF  00 FF FF 00  FF FF 00 FF  FF 00 FF FF   ..............
│000000A0  00 FF FF 00  FF FF 00 FF  FF 00 FF FF  00 FF FF 00   ..............
│000000B0  FF FF 00 FF  FF 00 FF FF  00 FF FF 00  FF FF 00 FF   ..............
│000000C0  FF 00 FF FF  00 FF FF 00  FF FF 00 FF  FF 00 FF FF   ..............
│000000D0  00 FF FF 00  FF FF 00 FF  FF 00 FF FF  00 FF FF 00   ..............
│000000E0  FF FF 00 FF  FF 00 FF FF  00 FF FF 00  FF FF 00 FF   ..............
│000000F0  FF 00 FF FF  00 FF FF 00  FF FF 00 FF  FF 00 FF FF   ..............
│00000100  00 FF FF 00  FF FF 00 FF  FF 00 FF FF  00 FF FF 00   ..............
│00000110  FF FF 00 FF  FF 00 FF FF  00 FF FF 00  FF FF 00 FF   ..............
│00000120  FF 00 FF FF  00 FF FF 00  FF FF 00 FF  FF 00 FF FF   ..............
│00000130  00 FF FF 00  FF FF 00 FF  FF 00 FF FF  00 FF FF 00   ..............
│00000140  FF FF 00 FF  FF 00 FF FF  00 FF FF 00  FF FF 00 FF   ..............
│00000150  FF 00 FF FF  00 FF FF 00  FF FF 00 FF  FF 00 FF FF   ..............
│00000160  00 FF FF 00  FF FF 00 FF  FF 00 FF FF  00 FF FF 00   ..............
│---   out.ppm        --0x0/0x1800F-------------------------------------------
```

Figure 3.1. A PPM file in hexedit. Bytes of the file are shown in hexadecimal in the middle columns. Row addresses are shown in the left. Any bytes that could be ASCII chars are displayed in the right-hand column.

Hex editors can also be used to hack a compiled program. Code is also data. If you have hard-coded strings in your compiled code they will show up in a hex editor, and can be easily modified to achieve all sorts of interesting effects.

If a hard-coded string is a keyword or password used to communicate with an external cloud service you can easily subvert the program's communication. I showed my Data Structures and Algorithms class how to hack game "achievements" systems by modifying keyword strings that were stored in the binary. The game would then tell the server that you had completed a difficult achievement when you had completed a very easy one.

Most hex editors will display each byte in the opened file as a hexadecimal code - 00 to FF. These are usually separated by spaces and grouped in columns and lines to make it easier to read.

We usually have a left-hand column showing the offset or address of the byte at the start of each line. This is usually also given in hex, and basically takes the role of a scrollbar to show you where you are viewing in the file.

Any byte values that correspond to printable ASCII values (hex values 20 for space to 7E for '~') are usually shown in a column to help you find the location of strings in the code. Other values are shown as dots. Note that this doesn't mean the bytes are actually ASCII characters - just that the values are in that range. You can also search for ASCII strings or byte sequences in the file.

In the above image (Figure 3.1) you can see that the ASCII header bytes at the start of the binary P6 PPM file are displayed as characters:

```
P6.256 127.255.
```

Note that any line feed (*0A*) characters are shown as dots, but the space (*20*) is represented as a space. We recall that this gives us the type of PPM - P6, the width of the image - 256 pixels, and the height - 127 pixels, and maximum colour channel value of 255, or FF in hex.

The rest of the file - the binary body - gives sequences of 3 bytes for RGB pixel colours. Our first colour sequence is FF 00 FF - full red, no green, and full blue (a bright purple pixel). If we open that image in an image editor it can be confirmed.

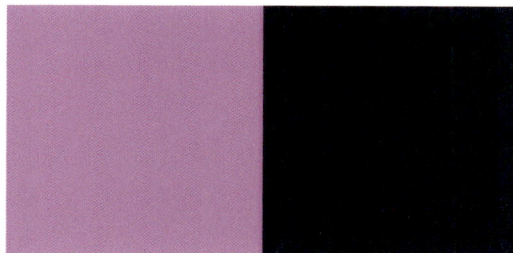

Figure 3.2. Opening the PPM image in an image editor such as GIMP will show that our assumption about purple pixels was correct.

This kind of process gives us a good basis for confirming that the file has been written correctly and has a structure that agrees with our assumptions. For reading and writing images and the like, it's often a good idea to create a test file with one red pixel at the top-left. This can tell you if you are reading the data from the correct location, or are somehow offset and there is more or less header than expected. You can do similar things for audio files.

You can also directly modify byte values with a hex editor. You can change the first body byte from FF to 00 to get a blue pixel in the top-left. This can be helpful for debugging, and sometimes is the easiest way to quickly patch small issues in software when the source code is not available.

In a Gamasutra article *More dirty coding tricks from game developers* by Brandon Sheffield (July 24, 2015), Ken Demarest recounts:

Back on the first Wing Commander we were getting an exception from our EMM386 memory manager when we exited the game. We'd clear the screen and a single line would print out, something like EMM386 Memory manager error. Blah blah blah.

We had to ship ASAP, so I hex edited the error in the memory manager itself to read:
Thank you for playing Wing Commander.

How to Work with Binary Files

Good binary file formats have:

1. Usually 2 or 3 ASCII bytes at the start of the file to indicate what type of file it is. This is sometimes referred to as a file's "magic number". Binary PPM has P and 6.
2. A well specified (in a document or website) header with fixed sizes for each variable.
3. The amount or count of data to read from the body.
4. The size of memory to allocate is given in the header.

If this is all true then we have a very easy process for reading the file:

1. Read the entire file into memory.
2. Inspect the first 2-3 bytes to determine file type.
3. Create a struct, exactly matching the file header memory layout, and create a pointer of this type and point it into memory.
4. Read header variables with our header pointer to find out how much memory to allocate, and other important details.
5. Decode the body data using the memory offset given by the header.
6. Use your hex editor to inspect the file as you write each part of your parser to spot any memory offset mistakes.
7. At each step be very careful to validate the data being read in case of a corrupted file or data layout mismatch.

Parsing a Binary PPM File

If we want to create a function that can read our binary PPM file it's not particularly difficult. Unfortunately binary PPM has an ASCII header, which means it has a varying number of bytes to represent numbers, and might have additional carriage return bytes at line endings. It's then easier to use typical ASCII file or string parsing functions to read this part of the file.

```c
FILE* fptr = fopen( filename, "rb" ); // 'rb' is 'read binary'
char type[2];
int32_t width, height, max_val;
int n = fscanf( fptr, "%c%c %i %i %i\n", &type[0], &type[1],
&width, &height, &max_val );
```

Avoid using %s to read strings as they have a risk of buffer overruns. I read exactly two %c characters. Avoiding buffer overruns is one reason why binary headers with fixed-sized fields are preferable.

Next we can determine the pixel data size in the body, allocate memory for it, and read it in.

```c
size_t pixel_data_sz    = width * height * 3; // 3 for RGB
uint8_t* pixel_data_ptr = malloc( pixel_data_sz );
fread( pixel_data_ptr, pixel_data_sz, 1, fptr );
fclose( fptr );
```

The PPM file and the pixel data is now in our program's memory and we can use it.

Reading Entire Binary Files

In some binary file formats the specification will give fixed byte sizes for each header variable. In that case it's convenient, and quicker, to read the entire file into memory first, then retrieve the header and the body from that memory. Validation is left off the following snippet to keep it short.

```c
struct file_record {
  void* data;
  size_t sz;
};

struct file_record read_file( const char* filename ) {
  struct file_record record;
  memset( &record, 0, sizeof( struct file_record ) );

  FILE* fp = fopen( filename, "rb" ); // 'read binary'
  if ( !fp ) { return record; } // error opening file
  fseek( fp, 0L, SEEK_END ); // jump to end-of-file (EOF)
  record.sz = (size_t)ftell( fp ); // byte position gives length
  record.data = malloc( record.sz );
  rewind( fp ); // jump back to start
  fread( record.data, record.sz, 1, fp ); // should return 1
  fclose( fp );
  return record;
}
```

Structs and Memory Alignment

The process of converting flat data, such as the record we have loaded from a file, into data structures in our program is called **deserialisation**. When writing a file we do the opposite - we convert our data structures to a 1D "array" of data (put it in series). This is called **serialisation**.

If we have a binary file loaded into memory, and the header is well specified, we can create a struct to mirror the header format. Then we can point a struct pointer at the binary data to conveniently pull out variables. BMP image files do have a fixed-sized header.

```
struct bmp_file_header* file_header_ptr = (struct
bmp_file_header*)record.data;
```

If you look up the BMP file format specification (Wikipedia has a good article) you can see we would write a `bmp_file_header` struct with exactly 14 bytes of variables. Offsets and sizes of variables are given in hex first, which gives you a hint of which tool we might use when working with this.

```
#pragma pack( push, 1 )  // pack byte-by-byte ... no padding
struct bmp_file_header {
  char file_type[2]; // 'char' -> we expect ASCII characters
  uint32_t file_sz;
  uint16_t reserved1;
  uint16_t reserved2;
  uint32_t image_data_offset;
};
#pragma pack( pop ) // revert to default byte-alignment
```

This looks pretty similar to the PPM header, except it has exact sizes for unsigned integers, and we also have some unusual preprocessor instructions.

Compilers can add blank memory padding between variables in structs to **align** the contents in memory. The compiler may add bytes such that struct variables *align to* 4 or 8 bytes of memory, for example. The amount of padding introduced depends on the compiler, the struct layout, and the compiler flags.

Any padding would break our struct pointer idea - the variables would be cast in the wrong places because the file's memory layout doesn't have this padding. You can add a compiler flag to disable struct padding, or you can add a hint in the code. The `#pragma pack( push, 1 )` and `#pragma pack( pop )` tell the compiler *"Don't do any packing alignment to structs, unions, or classes inside here!"* These preprocessor instructions should work on recent versions of all compilers the same way.

This approach lets us access variables from memory by name, like `file_header_ptr->image_data_offset`, or check all the values in the header clearly by inspecting our struct pointer in a debugger. When you have the struct pointer, confirm the values assigned to each variable match the values in the file. Use your hex editor and the offsets from the file format spec. You should be able to easily find and see the 1-byte magic number variables for the file type in both the debugger and the hex editor. It's quite common to make a mistake like forgetting a variable in the struct, and then the values of all subsequent struct variables will be wrong. Your hex editor can help you confirm the mistake. Variables larger than 1 byte are stored in file memory according to the **endianness** (see next section) of the file, which can be surprising the first time you use a hex editor.

With padding disabled we can also `fwrite()` a struct to a binary file. If it doesn't quite line up correctly we would bring up our hex editor and see where our struct variable sizes disagree with the values in a correctly laid out example file. This is a pretty typical method for creating file readers and writers, and a common use of a hex editor.

Endianness

- Not a complex technical term - it's a reference to a dispute in the story *Gulliver's Travels* by Jonathan Swift (1726), about which end of an egg to start eating from.
- If you have a 4-byte integer, in **little-endian** systems the numerically smallest byte is stored first (at the lower address). If you write an integer with the value of 1 to a binary file, your hex editor will either show
`01 00 00 00` (little-endian), or
`00 00 00 01` (**big-endian**).
If you are only writing single-byte values it doesn't make any difference.
- Endianness is no longer an important consideration for most binary data I/O (input/output) - almost all modern computers have standardised on little-endian memory and file I/O. This doesn't stop people bringing it up on every Stack Overflow post about file I/O! You are fine to assume little-endian order these days for reading and writing binary files. You can write custom code later if and when you need to work with an exotic big-endian-only system or its files.
- The most notable exception to this is socket-level networking, which can require big-endian binary data. In most cases conversion is handled by the underlying socket or networking library used.
- Some sections of binary file formats may be specified in big-endian order - check the specification!

Tips and Common Problems

- Parsing a file part-by-part with many disk access functions can be quite slow, but sometimes it is still the most convenient option.
- You can read the entire file to memory with one `fread()`, and parse from memory instead, which can be very convenient for some binary file formats, and is usually faster.
- It's also possible to **map** a file's disk memory into the program's memory space. This requires operating system-specific calls such as `mmap()` on Unix systems. This can be faster than standard file reading operations.
- Many commonly-used file formats are very poorly designed, and have ambiguous specifications, specifications that don't match common use, many diverging versions of the format to handle, excessive file size bloat, or are otherwise inefficient to parse.
- Reading and writing structs to and from files is unreliable unless you disable struct padding (byte alignment) when compiling.
- Using `#pragma pack( push, 1)` disables struct padding but breaks the alignment of your variables on memory. This may adversely affect the performance of your program on some CPU architectures or cause unexpected behaviour. If you intend your code to run on more than typical desktop processors, then this may not be a suitable option for you.
- If `#pragma pack` is unsuitable, the `offsetof()` macro can be used to retrieve the byte offset of a named variable within a struct.
- To get integers with exact bit sizes like **uint8_t** include the `stdint.h` header. This is commonly used in professional software to ensure that the size of the integer or data type used by the computer system matches the size used in the file. It's a good idea to replace all your integer data types with explicit sizes where they are going to be serialised or deserialised to and from files.
- Each file access function returns a value that should be validated - the number of variables scanned, the number of bytes read, etc. Your program

should be able to gracefully handle a corrupted file, or a file that was moved or deleted whilst being accessed.

- File reading and writing functions, especially offset into allocated memory, are a major reliability and security vulnerability of C and C++. You should consider using a **fuzzer** (see Chapter 9 - *Fuzz Testing with AFL*) to find the weak points in your file parsing routines.
- To test your image file functions you could modify the pixel memory and write out a new file. Does it open correctly in a range of image editors? Do the image file sizes match? Can you also read images created by other software?
- You can use the Unix cmp command-line utility to check if two binary files are the same. This is useful for testing read/write function pairs are consistent.

4 Interactive Debuggers

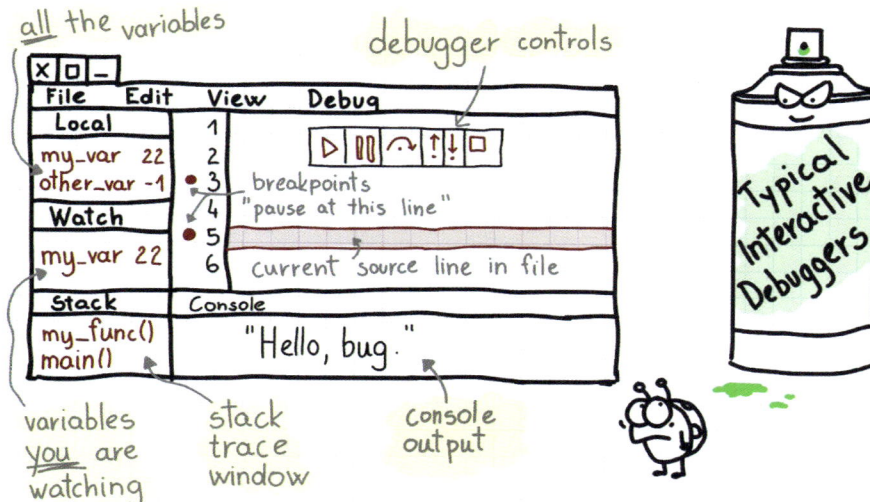

Figure 4.1. A typical interactive debugger lets you pause your program at **breakpoints**, **step** through code one line at a time, and use a **watch list** to see your variables change value.

Why Use Interactive Debuggers

It's a good exercise to be able to *walk* through a segment of your code on paper, to make sure you understand how the values in variables change after each instruction. This is what an interactive debugger does, except it works on your program while it is running, and gives you the exact values stored in variables at each step.

Interactive debuggers are one of your most useful development tools.

- Find out what conditions led up to a program crash.
- Find out why code doesn't work the way you expect it to.

- Step through **someone else's** spaghetti code to help learn how it works.
- Step through your own spaghetti code to help learn how it works.
- Walk through critical sections of code to inspect for inefficiencies or risks.

Can you do this by sprinkling `printf()`? Yes, it can be quicker sometimes, and it turns out some very experienced programmers don't like interactive debuggers, although `printf` debugging can get very tedious. If you haven't learned how to use an interactive debugger yet - do so - more tools means more options for you, and they can be extra helpful for people learning. It's still useful to be able to get a **backtrace** of your program after a crash, and we will look at how your debugger can do this too.

Some Interactive Debuggers

The most commonly used debuggers are:

- GDB is the GNU project debugger (pairs with GCC) - very commonly used on GNU/Linux.
- LLDB is the LLVM project debugger (pairs with the Clang compiler) - the default on Apple.
- The Microsoft Visual Studio IDE has a very powerful integrated debugger.

LLDB has an interface almost exactly the same as GDB, just as Clang mirrors GCC's interface.

If you enter `gdb` or `gcc` in a macOS terminal, after you install Xcode, it will actually run `lldb` and `clang`, respectively.

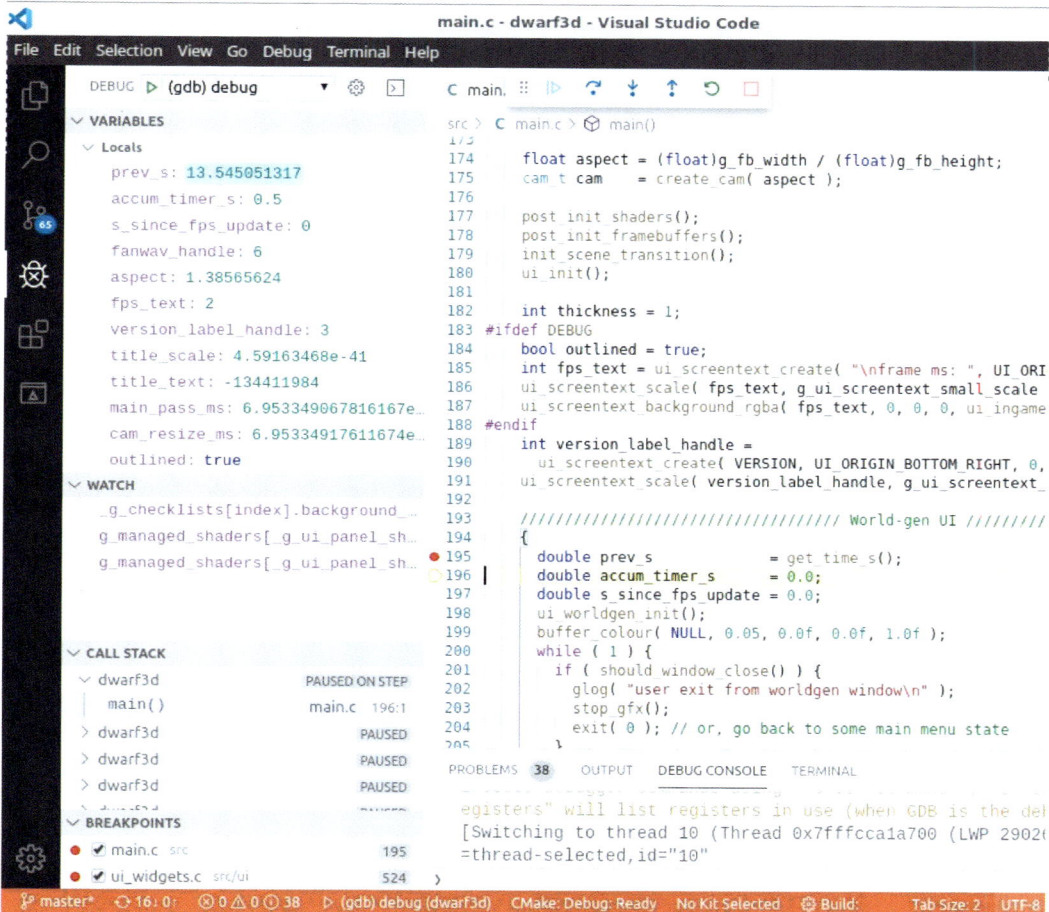

Figure 4.2. Microsoft Visual Studio Code using its C/C++ plug-in to act as a front end to the GDB debugger on a Linux system. It supports several debuggers and platforms.

GDB and LLDB have interactive command-line interfaces. You can do everything in the terminal if you like, sometimes that's convenient, but usually it's much easier to use a graphical front-end to the debuggers. Microsoft's open-source Visual Studio Code editor has a decent GDB/LLDB front-end, and it is my main debugging tool on all platforms these days. Xcode, other IDEs, and some stand-alone tools also give you a debugger front-end, although many are not very fast or reliable.

How to use a Debugger

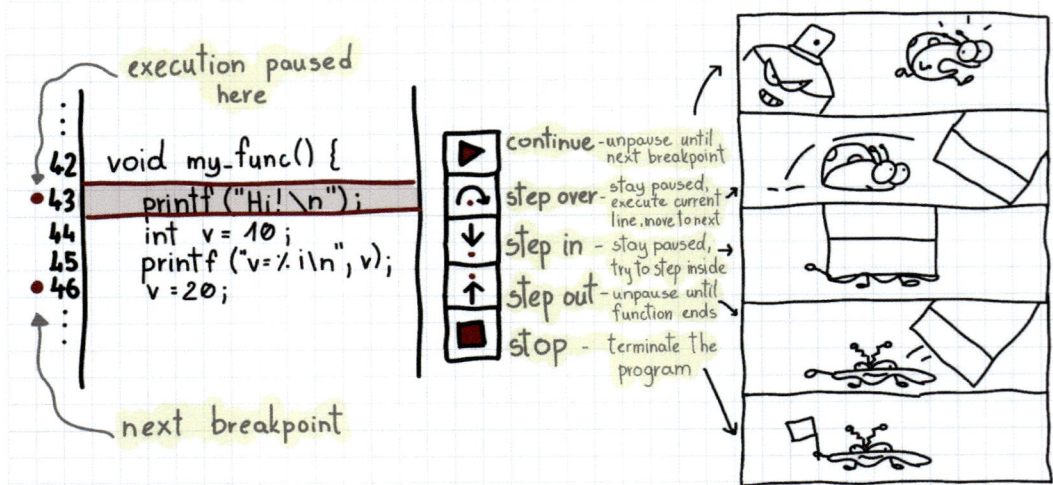

Figure 4.3. Click in the margin to set breakpoints at lines in your code. Use debugger controls to start debugging. Execution pauses on breakpoints.

1. Compile a **debug build** of your program. In an IDE this is usually a drop-down box you can find that switches between debug and release builds. For GCC and Clang you add the -g flag to your compiler. This adds debug symbols to your build, which lets the debugger know what all your file and function names are. Otherwise it may not debug your program at all, or with very limited information.

```
gcc -g -o my_program main.c other_file.c
```

2. Set a **breakpoint** in your code. In an IDE this is usually done by clicking in the margin on the left hand side of your code. It will be shown as a **big red dot**. Put the breakpoint somewhere next to an actual code instruction that will execute like printf("Hello, world!\n"), not a blank line, a declaration, or a function name.

3. Most IDEs will have a big green arrow button, a button with an icon of a bug, or a Debug menu that gives you the option to run your program in debugging mode. Visual Studio Code will ask you to tell it the path to your debugger and your program in a config file first. *Hit the button*! Your program should run as normal, and pause at the line of your breakpoint, without executing the instruction.

4. *When paused*

     a. You can usually **hover** your mouse over variable names to see what value they currently hold.
     b. You usually get a panel of in-scope **local** variables and their current values.
     c. You can see the stack of functions currently open in a **stack trace** window.
     d. You can right-click a variable name in your code, and add it to a **watch list**, to track the value it holds.
     e. You can **step over** to execute the current instruction, and pause on the next instruction.
     f. You can **step in** to have the debugger step to the first instruction inside a function call.
     g. You can **step out** to continue execution and pause on the instruction after the current function call.
     h. You can unpause and **continue** execution until the next breakpoint is hit.

5. When not paused you should have a button to **pause** execution. This can be handy to somewhat randomly find functions that consume a lot of processing time, and start debugging them.

6. If the program crashes the stack trace gives you the **backtrace** - a trail of fingerprints (function calls) you need to reconstruct the crime scene, and find out what went wrong. If it's not clear, you can start adding breakpoints and `assert()` statements to catch your problem on a subsequent run.

Quick Command-Line Backtrace

If your program crashes when you're not using an IDE, you can run e.g. GDB on the command line, and deliberately try to crash it again.

```
gdb ./my_program
gdb) run
Program received signal SIGSEGV, Segmentation fault.
function_that_crashed () at .\main.c:6
6                   int value = *ptr; // should crash here.
gdb) bt
#0  function_that_crashed () at .\main.c:6
#1  0x0000000000401589 in some_intermediate_function () at
.\main.c:11
#2  0x00000000004015a2 in main () at .\main.c:15
gdb) q
```

If your program takes command line arguments, put them after 'run' in the GDB terminal.

```
gdb) run first_arg second_arg
```

The backtrace printed by the bt command gives the path taken through the program, with function names, file names, and line numbers, that lead up to the crash. This is often all you need to find a fail point in the code.

- You can also print the source code near the crash with list.
- And print the values of any in-scope variable with p my_variable_name.
- Within GDB, type help for more commands.
- Outside of GDB type man gdb to access the manual.

Using Core Dumps and JIT Debugging

The down-side to the above method of getting a backtrace is that you need to successfully crash the program again.

With Visual Studio you can enable JIT (*Just In Time*) Debugging in the project properties settings. When the program crashes it will pop up a dialogue asking if you'd like to jump to a debugger. This takes you to the line that crashed, where you'll have a stack trace and can inspect the variables at the time of the crash. That should give you enough detail to find most crashing bugs.

On Linux and macOS you can enable core dumps in the terminal. When a program crashes it will then write a file containing all the program data at the time of the crash. By default the size limit for crash dumps is set to 0. To find the current limit enter `ulimit -c`. Set this to `unlimited` to enable core dumps.

```
ulimit -c unlimited
```

These can be very large files. You'll need to clean them up or disable core dump writing when you're no longer testing programs.

```
$ ./my_program
Segmentation fault: 11 (core dumped)
```

On macOS these files are written into `/cores/`, and you can start a GDB or LLDB session with your core dump. My core dump was called `/cores/core.4287`. Once in the debugger you can get a backtrace. It will also tell you the signal fired when the program crashed.

```
$ lldb ./my_program -c /cores/core.4287
```

```
(lldb) target create "./a.out" --core "/cores/core.4287"
Core file '/cores/core.4287' (x86_64) was loaded.
(lldb) bt
* thread #1, stop reason = signal SIGSTOP
  * frame #0: 0x000000010d33ef3f a.out`function_that_crashed at main.c:43:14
    frame #1: 0x000000010d33ef69 a.out`some_intermediate_function at main.c:48:2
    frame #2: 0x000000010d33ef84 a.out`main at main.c:52:2
    frame #3: 0x00007fff7ad253d5 libdyld.dylib`start + 1
    frame #4: 0x00007fff7ad253d5 libdyld.dylib`start + 1
```

Figure 4.4. Typing `bt` in my LLDB session gave me the backtrace. I get line numbers where it crashed too, since my program was built with debug symbols.

We can use the debugger to get more information from the core near the crash. We can also look at the source code of the crashing function, and get the values of variables to find the cause of the crash. The list command prints source code. With GDB we can use `print ptr` to inspect the value of `ptr`, which should reveal the address `0x00` - or NULL.

```
(lldb) list function_that_crashed
File: /Users/anton/projects/howto_pvt/book_testing/04_deliberate_crash/main.c
   37
   38   #include <stdio.h>
   39
   40   int* ptr = NULL;
   41
   42   void function_that_crashed() {
   43           int value = *ptr; // should crash here. dereferencing a null poi
nter.
   44           printf( "value %i\n", value );
   45   }
   46
   47   void some_intermediate_function() {
   48           function_that_crashed();
   49   }
   50
(lldb) frame variable ptr
(int *) ptr = 0x0000000000000000
```

Figure 4.5. By listing the code of the crashing function we see a pointer on the crashing line. Getting the value of that variable we see `0x00`, which is a NULL pointer. Dereferencing a NULL pointer caused our crash.

Tips and Common Problems

- Remember to build a debug version of your program, and run that same debug version in the debugger, or the tools won't give you much information. If you see lots of question marks where function names should be, or the debugger doesn't stop at a breakpoint - this is probably why.
- Most debuggers will let you set a **conditional breakpoint**, that only stops the debugger if some condition relating the variables in your code is satisfied like `number_of_iterations > 10000` to find problems that happen later in your program. In Visual Studio Code *right-click* instead of left-clicking when placing a breakpoint in the margin.
- Some debuggers will also let you set a **data breakpoint**, that stops the debugger if a variable from your watch list changes value. The CLion IDE calls these **watchpoints**.
- Some debuggers will let you set a **logpoint**. This is a breakpoint that prints text instead of halting execution. It can be used to *inject a printf* in a program that you are debugging but cannot stop to modify.
- It can be misleading to inspect the value of a variable when it hasn't been initialised yet.
- If you've added an array to the watch list, but it's only added the first variable, you should be able to change that to a drop down list of elements. Each IDE has a slightly different syntax for setting that in the watch list.
- The Visual Studio debugger lets you "*go to the disassembly*" during a debugging session, and step through asm (assembly code) corresponding to your higher-level code instructions.
- Visual Studio, and some other IDEs, maintain different project settings for the release and debug builds - you may need to go and replicate some of your project settings, libraries used, and include paths in settings panels to get the debug build to compile.

- If you want to debug into libraries you are using, some libraries will supply debug builds of the libraries. You don't normally need these to debug your program.
- If you can't step in to a function, it's probably because it comes from a file, or a library, that was not built with debugging symbols.
- Most watch lists will let you switch display of values to hexadecimal, which can be useful for some types of data like colour codes.
- You can use most watch lists to convert hex values to decimal for you - add a hex value, e.g. `0xFF`, rather than a variable name, to the watch list.
- You can do the same trick for getting the ASCII value for a character e.g. `'q'`.
- Having a friend or colleague sit with you when debugging a tricky problem can often be really helpful to spot something you missed, especially if they ask lots of pesky questions, and you can tell them how you think it should work.
- You can also do this by yourself out loud - it's called *rubber ducking* (explaining your code to a rubber duck on your desk).
- *"The debugger skipped over my breakpoint!"* This can happen if the compiler optimised out a chunk of your code that it determined did nothing, you're not running a debug build, or the code you're editing is not building to the same `.exe` file that you're debugging!
- Visual Studio has a full memory inspection panel where you can look up the address of any variables during debugging and find what values are set there in hex, and the byte values in memory of anything nearby.
- Some debuggers also provide diagnostic tools that can tell you at any point the CPU and memory used by the program.
- Debuggers will allow you to attach to an already running program, instead of launching it from the debugger. If you know the process ID of the program (see Chapter 13 for how to list process IDs), with GDB

```
gdb -p 1234
```

- Running `gdbserver` allows `gdb` on a remote machine to debug your program over a network.

5 Performance Profilers

Profilers analyse a program to help direct performance optimisation efforts. Profilers output a **profile** - tables or spreadsheets and sometimes charts or annotated code.

Why Use Profilers

Profilers typically analyse

- Duration - *"What are my most time-hungry functions?"*
- Frequency - *"What are my most commonly called functions?"*

Performance optimisation can

- Reduce the time to get your program's job done.
- Reduce overall system resource usage, to be kind to other apps or lower system requirements.
- Improve performance *spikes* and remove stutters, slowness and perceived latency (responsiveness) from the user experience.
- Reduce power consumption or battery usage of your app.
- This also helps you to understand and simplify your code, and write more efficient code in the future.

There are three basic profiler types

1. **Instrumenting** profiler - add hooks into your code to collect data.
2. Statistical **sampling** profiler - usually an external program that inspects your program's **call stack** of functions at a regular interval.
3. Some use a mixture of both.

Some profilers will let you set the sampling frequency. Note that this means a profile is usually not an exact analysis. Instrumenting your code will also change the performance of your program, which adds a significant bias to analysis.

Profilers typically record events in a **trace** over a run, or successive runs of your program.

After collecting data, you get an analysis break-down - the **profile**:

- A **flat profile** - The count, or frequency, each function was called during the trace, and the average or total time spent in each function.
- A **call graph** - the paths through functions where most program time is spent.

Some tools also provide

- Nice "heat" or flame graph visualisations.
- Interactive **drill-down** views through function calls for more detail.
- A trace timeline view to show when performance spikes occur.
- Memory used over the trace.

How to Analyse a Program

Manual Instrumentation and Sampling

You may add timers to your code, before and after a code block of interest. I do this during graphics and games development for major parts of the update loop, and display the times on-screen. This lets you see the relative cost of different parts as your scene changes. I don't do this every iteration, but take a sample on a fixed interval. You can also log this to a file to build a profile.

The basic timers in C are not very precise, and you need to use an operating system-specific function to get a reliable high-precision timer.

- On Windows `QueryPerformanceCounter()` is a good choice.
- On Linux `clock_gettime( CLOCK_MONOTONIC, &t )` gives you a

nanosecond timer. Monotonic clocks are not affected by things like date or time changes on the system, so are reliable timers.

- On macOS `mach_absolute_time()` can be used with `mach_timebase_info()`.
- In C++11 or newer there is a cross-platform `std::chrono` API which provides high-resolution timers. The highest resolution clock is accessed with `std::chrono::high_resolution_clock::now()`. You can check if the high resolution clock is also monotonic with `is_steady()`. The API has functions for comparing times and returning a result in seconds or milliseconds.

Similarly, you can occasionally pause your program during debugging to see where it stops. The most frequently used function bottlenecks may be revealed.

Gprof

Gprof is one of the oldest and most widely used profilers. It is a hybrid instrumenting/sampling profiler, and pairs with GCC and Clang. If you are using C or C++, start with Gprof as a first profiler, because it's quite good, and also introduces you to some of the issues with profiling.

1. Ask GCC or Clang to instrument your code by providing the `-pg` flag to the compiler.

```
gcc -pg -o myprogram main.c
```

- You can also do a profiling build that adds annotations to a copy of your source code with `-a`.

2. Run the program, do normal stuff for a while.

```
./my_program
```

This spits out an output log file called `gmon.out`.

3. Run gprof on the log to produce results tables.

```
gprof ./my_program gmon.out > results.txt
```

4. Open `results.txt` in a text editor.

In the example output below, I have a profiled program that contains functions that call other functions, with some pointless loops to occupy time. The functions are called `parent()`, `child()`, `grandchild()`, and `great_grandchild()`.

The Flat Profile

The flat profile lists all the functions called in your program by the time spent in each, individually and cumulatively.

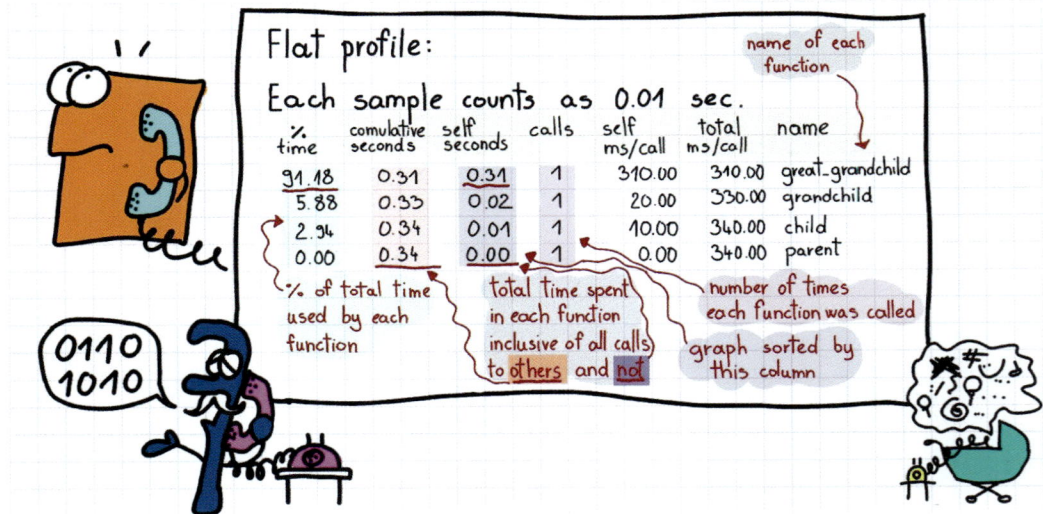

Figure 5.1. We can see that `great_grandchild()` is by far our most expensive function with 91% of program time spent in it, and it was only called once.

The Call Graph

The Call Graph helps spot expensive chains or graphs of functions calling functions, that together add up to a high cost.

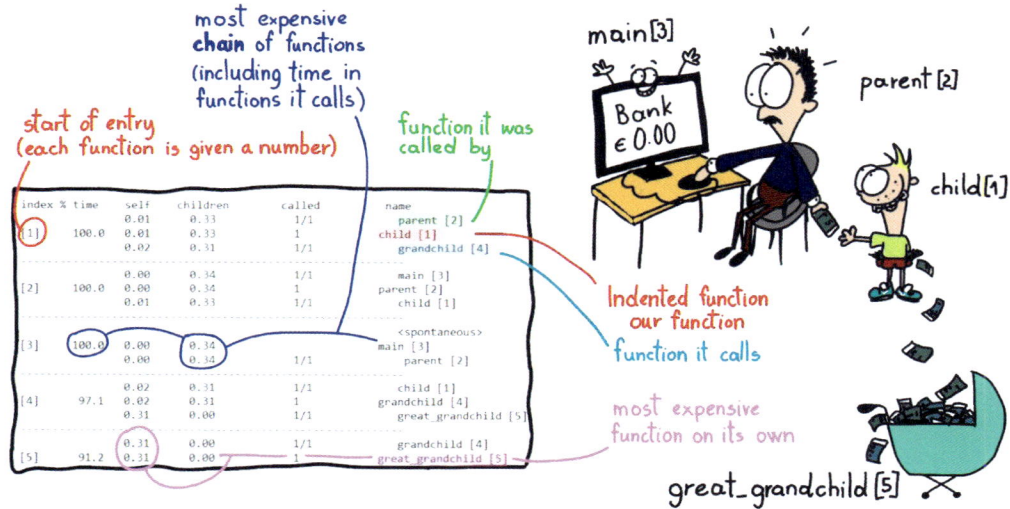

most expensive **chain** of functions (including time in functions it calls)

start of entry (each function is given a number)

function it was called by

```
index % time   self   children   called    name
               0.01   0.33       1/1           parent [2]
[1]    100.0   0.01   0.33       1         child [1]
               0.02   0.31       1/1           grandchild [4]

               0.00   0.34       1/1           main [3]
[2]    100.0   0.00   0.34       1         parent [2]
               0.01   0.33       1/1           child [1]

                                               <spontaneous>
[3]    100.0   0.00   0.34                 main [3]
               0.00   0.34       1/1           parent [2]

               0.02   0.31       1/1           child [1]
[4]    97.1    0.02   0.31       1         grandchild [4]
               0.31   0.00       1/1           great_grandchild [5]

               0.31   0.00       1/1           grandchild [4]
[5]    91.2    0.31   0.00       1         great_grandchild [5]
```

main [3]

Bank € 0.00

parent [2]

child [1]

Indented function our function

function it calls

most expensive function on its own

great_grandchild [5]

Figure 5.2. We read in this call graph that the graph of `child()->grandchild()->great_grandchild()` *accounts for 100% of program time. Time spent in the* `main()->parent()` *part is insignificant.*

Other profilers have a similar process and have standardised on the same sort of profile output as Gprof. Gprof's instrumented builds slow down your program considerably, which can limit its usefulness for some cases.

How to use the Profile to Optimise

We can try to optimise performance **bottlenecks** you may spot at the top of your flat profile and call graph

1. **Short, frequently called utility functions** - consider **inlining**.
2. **Long functions** - look at the code - can it be simplified?
3. **Chains of many tiny functions** - hard to analyse and add up individually - look at the **call graph** to help guide optimisation.

Inlined code is duplicated in your compiled program, rather than being reused in a function call. This avoids function call overhead, and can be suitable for very small functions that are used everywhere. C++ and C99 have the `inline` keyword for functions. You can use a macro for one-liners.

Some functions do a lot of heavy lifting and need to be time-expensive. Our goal here is to find code that can be simplified, and check for unexpected costs. In expensive functions you can think about algorithmic complexity - look for **nested loops**.

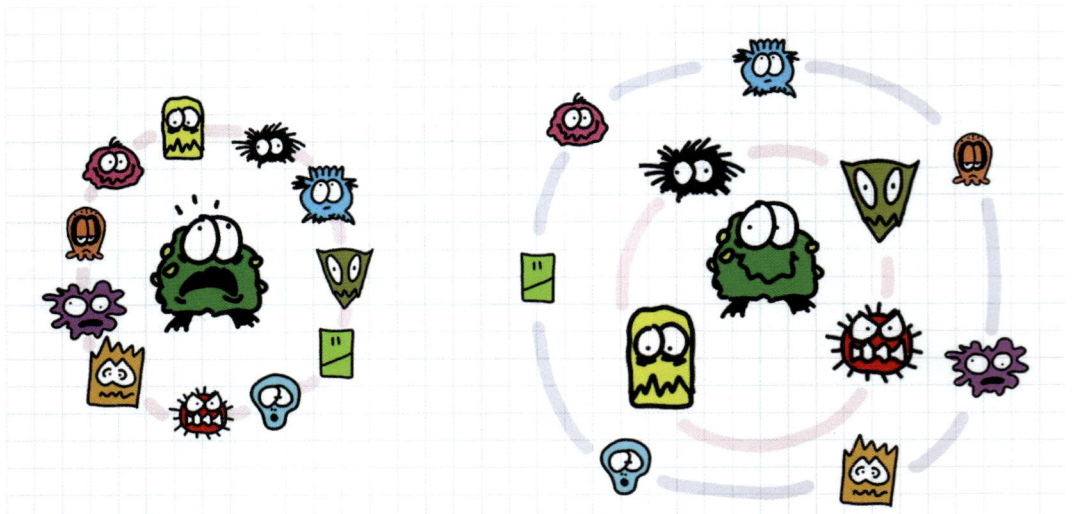

Figure 5.3. *In a monster update function every monster looks at every other monster. Can we simplify this by only looking at a subset of other monsters?*

Perhaps a game's monsters, (Figure 5.3), use an update **loop** over a long list of *n* monsters. Monsters are moved in the update function, but shouldn't collide. Does *each monster also look **at every other** monster*? That suggests an $O(n^2)$ complexity algorithm. Can it be reduced to $O(n)$? Perhaps by checking a much smaller subset of nearby monsters instead of the entire list of monsters each time.

You may also spot expensive code paths in the call graph that have deep call chains of functions that are not expensive individually. Are there too many very small functions? Would these be easier to reason about in one, longer function? Perhaps a small generic function is used everywhere, but using smaller, more specialised functions can improve overall performance and clarity. Can a recursive function be replaced with a loop?

Sometimes expensive code paths are through stacks of libraries, and often you can make the biggest performance improvements to your program by replacing libraries with small hand-written utility functions.

Profile again after trying some improvements

- Often you've made it perform *worse*!
- Optimisation is hard but it is worth reasoning about as a regular part of your development cycle.
- Try your program on different computers!
- Read literature and ask experts - is there a data structure or algorithm for this?
- Know how the hardware works, and what it likes - *Are we misusing the cache or causing page faults? Is some of the work being done on the GPU (graphics processing unit)?*
- Inspect the assembly code of critical functions.

Sometimes the answer is *"No, don't optimise further!"*. Over-optimised code means

- Lose useful features.
- Code becomes more expensive to maintain - many architecture-specific branches.
- Lose clarity/simplicity.
- Potential gains are too small to justify the amount of work.
- Optimised versions are too hardware-specific, and less portable.

Optimise-or-not decisions

- What are the target machines?
- Who needs to work on this code - can it be easily handed over?
- What is the user's perception of performance?
- Quality impact versus time to implement with respect to deadlines or impact on product iteration time.

Other Profilers

Very Sleepy (Windows)

- The same principles as Gprof except no profiling-specific build required.
- Download from http://www.codersnotes.com/sleepy/.
- Attaches to any running process.
- Run a build of your program that has debug symbols otherwise you get no function names or line numbers.
- Attach to your program, then start recording a trace.
- It can profile MinGW GCC builds, but you may need to compile with `-gdwarf-2 -g` for it to see function names.

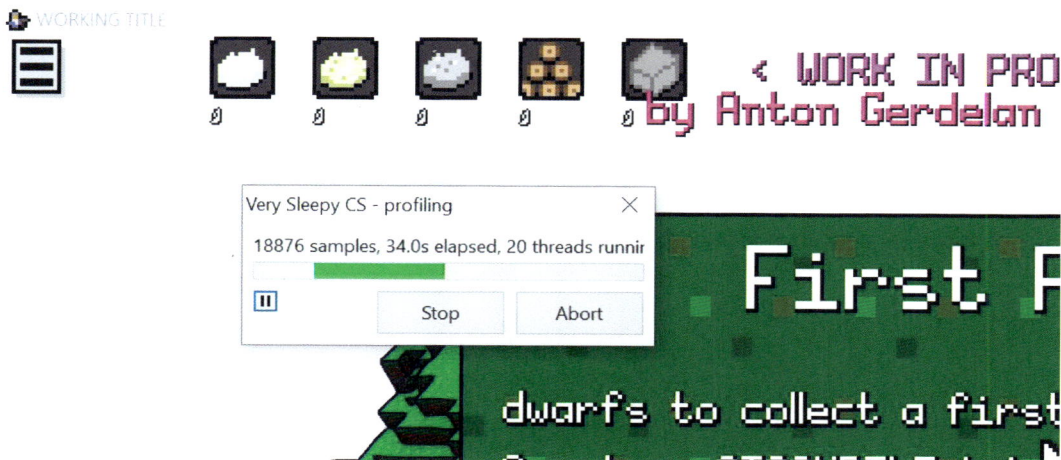

Figure 5.4. Pictured we see Very Sleepy has started recording a trace - it shows the small window overlaying the game project in the background - and we can stop it when we like.

Very Sleepy lists running processes, and the big advantage is that we can easily start recording profiling data from a program that is already running. I was able to attach it to a game project. We can also interactively pause or stop recording a trace, so that we only record a period of interest to us.

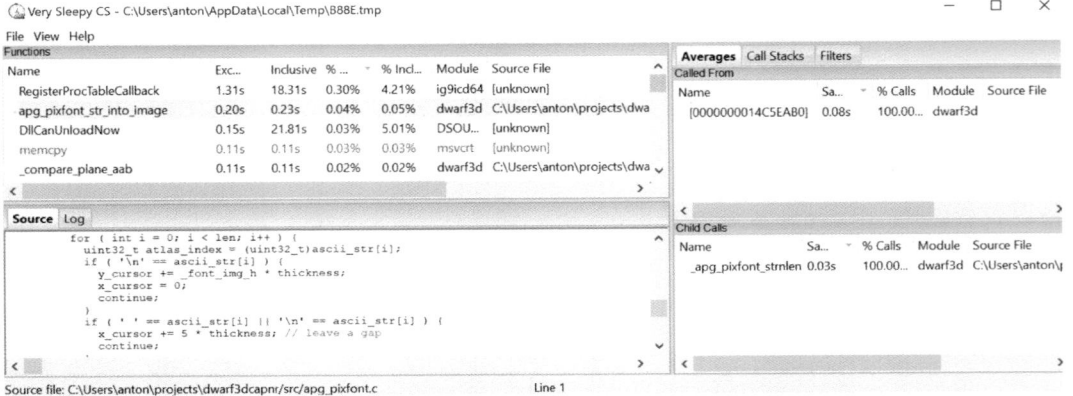

Figure 5.5. After I stopped recording the profile in the previous image Very Sleepy presents the profile results. It shows the most expensive function in my trace - `apg_pixfont_str_into_image()`, and gives a view into the function's source code.

If Very Sleepy can find the debug symbols then it presents call frequency, time, and parent and child calls for each function. We also get the functions and files of expensive functions in our code as well as a source code view. The ease of use makes Very Sleepy a very handy tool for Windows programming, without needing to prepare a special build or instrumenting code. I have Very Sleepy pinned to the Windows taskbar for convenience.

Perf (Linux)

Perf is a very powerful, low-overhead Linux profiler.

```
sudo perf record -ag -F 99 ./my_program
sudo perf report
```

Perf usually requires super user permissions to run. When recording `-a` profiles all CPUs, `-g` generates a call graph that you can interactively browse, and `-F 99` samples at 99Hz.

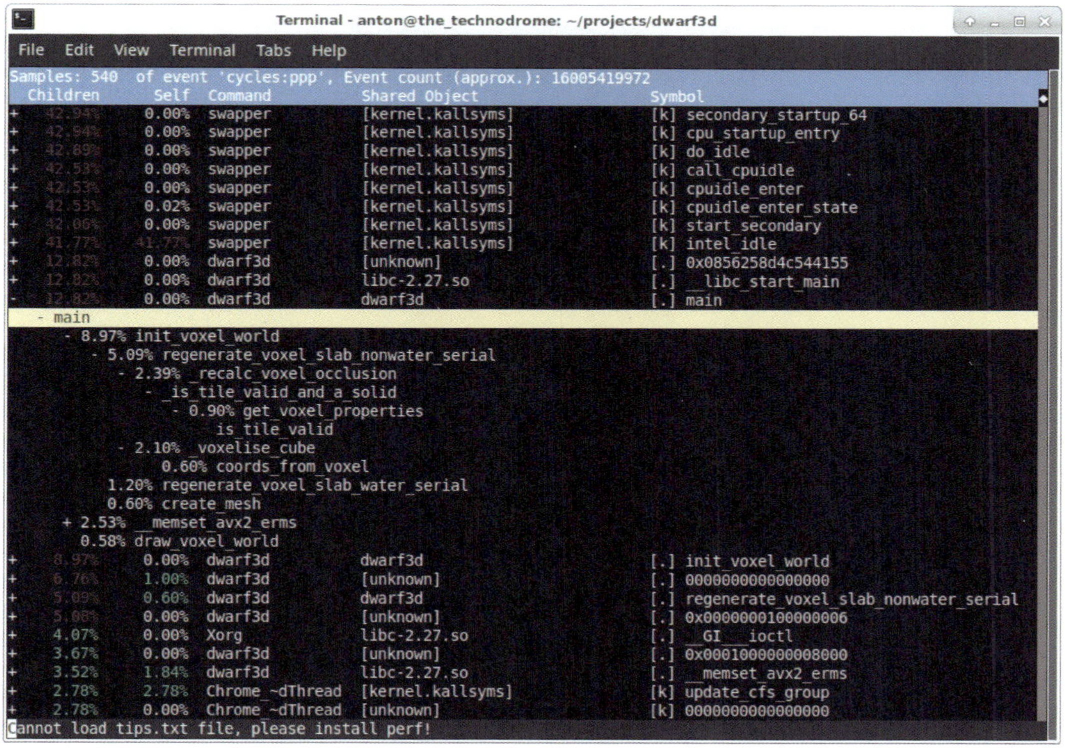

Figure 5.6. Drilling down in a call graph in a perf report.

The report is an interactive multi-view program that can browse the function call frequencies, and also annotate source code with time percentages for each function, disassembled to asm.

Perf can also be used to time a process with `sudo perf stat`, and be run as an interactive performance monitor, listing the most CPU-expensive functions of your code currently running, with `perf top`.

Remotery

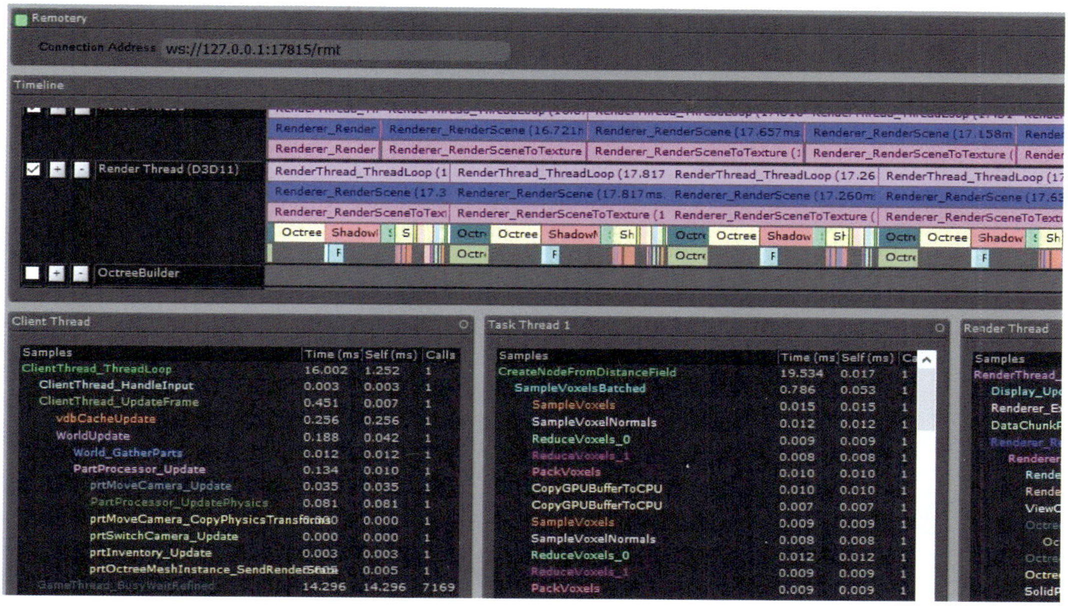

Figure 5.7. A web browser gives a live display of Remotery's call graph with a function timeline across several threads of a video game. Cropped to fit. Image courtesy of Don Williamson.

Remotery https://github.com/Celtoys/Remotery is an instrumenting C profiler by Don Williamson that has a single C file that you include in your C or C++ project. You then add hooks into your code. Remotery uses a web browser to display the call graph and a function call timeline. It connects to a web browser using web sockets, where you can interactively visualise your program's profile as it runs.

- Runs with pretty much every operating system, including mobile devices.
- Easy to build into your project and run.
- Interactive timeline view.
- Can also profile GPU events with several graphics APIs.
- Can debug remote or embedded devices over a network.

Microsoft Visual Studio (Windows)

Recent releases of Visual Studio IDE have a great integrated code profiler tool set under the `Analyze` menu. It has all the same profile data as Gprof, but also provides an interactive report with a *Hot Path* slice of the call graph to help highlight bottlenecks. It also has an interactive timeline to filter profile results. This can be used to help drill down into performance spikes that may cause a bad user experience.

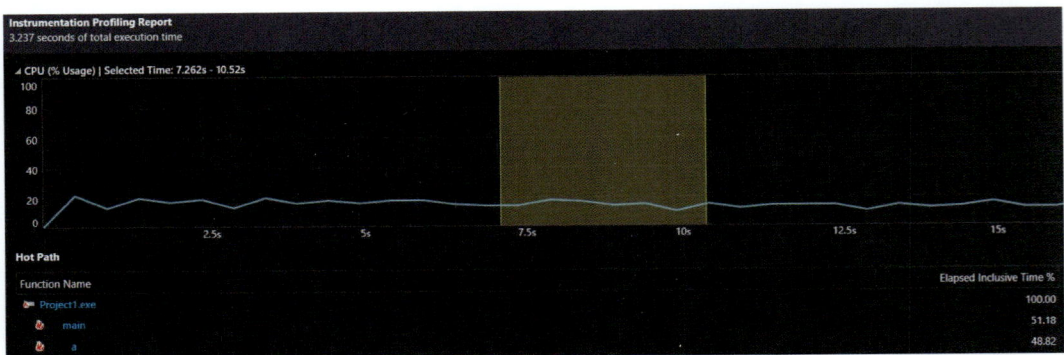

Figure 5.8. The Visual Studio profiler can interactively filter its profile by a selection of the trace timeline.

In addition to the integrated profiler, the Intel *VTune* profiler has been a leading commercial profiler, and is now available as a free plug-in for Visual Studio. https://software.intel.com/en-us/vtune

Instruments (macOS)

Xcode installs with a suite of utilities called *Instruments*.

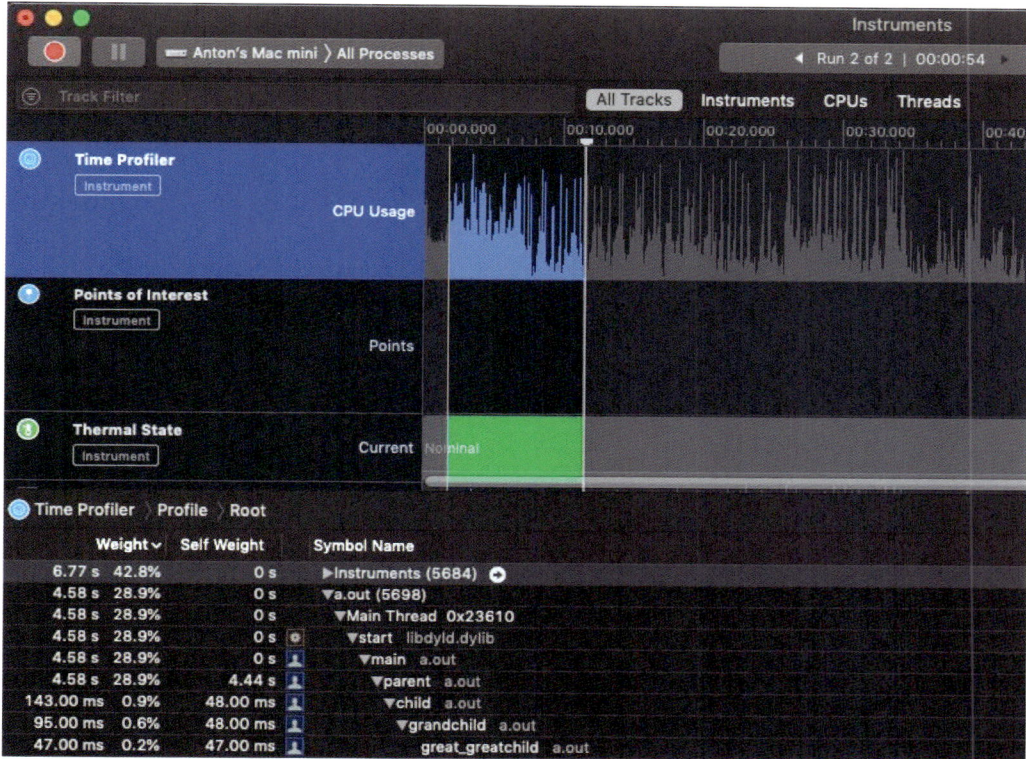

Figure 5.9. Instruments has recorded all the processes on my system, and I'm examining the Call Graph tree for the functions in my program (a.out).

- If you CTRL+click on the Xcode app icon you can launch Instruments independently.
- The *Time Profiler* option gives you a profiler, with a scoped timeline similar to Visual Studio.
- You can have the profiler record all processes currently running on the system, including your program.
- You can explore the *Call Graph* tree to get details of the cost of functions within your program for a slice of the recorded timeline.

Tips and Common Problems

- If you need finer-grained statistics about the frequency that each code **instruction** is called, you can use the GNU gcov tool together with gprof. Gcov is usually used to produce **test coverage** reports - you would run it with your test program to find code not called by the test suites. It outputs a copy of your source code with an exact count of calls annotated beside each instruction. https://gcc.gnu.org/onlinedocs/gcc/Gcov-Intro.html
- The performance of debug and release builds, or at different levels of compiler optimisation, can vary hugely. Know which version you are profiling!
- Some instrumenting compilers require special compiler flags in order to work.
- Blocking I/O operations like print-outs may be excluded from profiler timing. Testing a profiler on a loop of print statements may produce unintuitive results!
- Disk accesses can be very time consuming. Can these be reduced, working from main memory instead?
- Agner Fog has a large collection of optimisation articles and resources. https://www.agner.org/optimize/

6 Build Systems

Building a program or library from several parts can be a little tricky, and some projects use a **build system** to help organise the different parts. Build systems compile and link a program or library from a list of files and dependencies.

You will come across many build systems in your career, and need to be familiar with a few. The most portable and longest-living projects tend to be the ones that require no build system at all.

Why Use a Build System

- Reduce build time by not recompiling files that haven't changed.
- Can be configured to create multiple builds of your program - release, debug, testing, 32-bit or 64-bit, builds for different platforms, and so on.
- Some check if required libraries are installed on the system. This is handy for shipping source code to be compiled by users.
- Meta-build systems can generate project files for any build system. This is handy for shipping library source code.

Catches with Build Systems

- There is no standard or universal build system for C.
- Some are tied to a particular IDE or tool suite. Most require developers to install their matching build system tools.
- Add significant complexity and boilerplate maintenance work.
- Are a dependency.

Choosing a Build System

A bad reason for choosing a build system is to avoid learning how to build projects from the command line. The command line should always be your first build system to consider. If your project can easily be compiled from the command line then anyone can easily drag your source files into their favourite build system too, which means your code is easy to distribute.

1. Compile directly from the command line.
2. When your command gets quite long write it into a shell or batch script.
3. When it gets more complex consider a Makefile.
4. If you are widely distributing complex code projects for multiple platforms and development environments then consider a meta-build system.
5. Put work into simplifying the build requirements of your project.

The following sections review building programs from the command line with GCC, then we will move those examples into a Makefile. Other compilers use almost the same instructions, with slightly different flags and options.

Linking a C Program with Multiple Source Files

To create a program from more than one source file you simply add those into the compilation command

```
gcc main.c second.c
```

- One file, and only one file, must contain a function called main().
- Symbols (variable and function names) are considered external by default during linking, which means they can be shared between files.
- But source files are compiled without knowing about any other files.
- To call a function in main.c that is defined in second.c you need to add a declaration of that function at the top of main.c. The compiler then trusts

that the linker will hook the call up to the definition later.

- The linker will fail if function names and global variables have the same name in different files: "*multiple definition of …*". To keep a symbol internal or private to a **translation unit** (compiled source code file) so this doesn't happen, put the `static` keyword in front of it. This is a good default to add for all functions and global variables that you don't intend to share between files.
- Header files are usually used to share declarations of functions between several files.
- If a header file is included more than once the declarations can appear to be multiply defined, which will stop the build. Add a header guard to the top of the header to stop this happening

```
#pragma once
```

This preprocessor directive should work on all recent compilers now. Otherwise the older approach is to open a header guard at the top of the file, using a unique name for the file.

```
#ifndef MY_HEADER_FILE_NAME_H_
#define MY_HEADER_FILE_NAME_H_
```

And then close it at the bottom of the file.

```
#endif
```

Linking a Library with a C Program

If your program links a static library add it to the compilation arguments.

```
gcc main.c static_library_name.a
```

If your program links a dynamic library, add it to the arguments to be passed to the linker.

```
gcc main.c -ldynamic_library_name
```

For Clang and GCC the naming convention for dynamic libraries usually does not include their filename extension. If the library filename starts with "lib", such as libm.so, that is also left off.

```
gcc main.c -lm
```

If your library is in a different folder you will need to supply the path to it. With Clang and GCC that is the -L flag.

```
gcc main.c -Lpath/to/lib/ -ldynamic_library_name
```

Library interface functions are usually declared in a header file. You will need to supply the paths to any header files in different locations with -I.

```
gcc main.c -Ipath/to/my/own/headers/ -Ipath/to/lib/headers/
-Lpath/to/lib/ -ldynamic_library_name
```

Make and Makefiles

Make is one of the most common, easily recognisable, and oldest build systems for C projects, and one of the simplest, but it has some *gotchas*.

- Originally a Unix tool, GNU Make is probably the most popular implementation of Make.
- You write a text file named `Makefile` for your project.
- Makefiles are build scripts, executed by a program called `make`.
- Type `make` from the command line to run the Makefile in the current directory.
- You can avoid recompiling files that haven't had changes.
- Some IDEs recognise and work with Makefiles.

I have a program that has 2 source files, and links in `libm`. On the command line I compile like this

```
gcc main.c two.c -lm
```

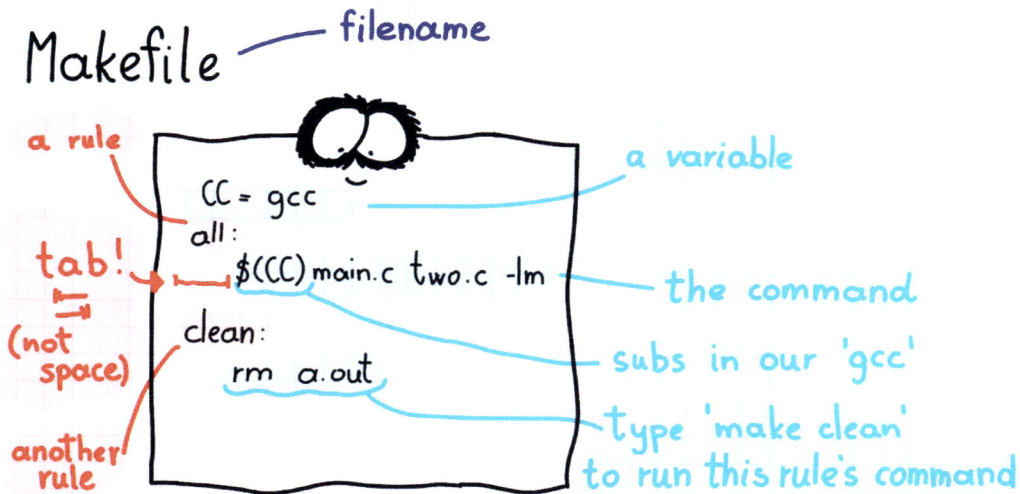

Figure 6.1. A Makefile and its plain-text contents, with rules and a variable.

- If you have the *make* program installed just type `make` and it will run the first rule in the file.
- You can also type `make`, followed by a rule name to run a specific rule.
- Most makefiles will have an 'all', 'clean', and 'install' rule, but you can use any rule names.
- The biggest *gotcha* with Makefiles is that commands (under rules), like `gcc main.c...` must be **indented with a tab**, and make will give an error if they are indented with anything else.
- If you type `make`, space then hit `Tab` some terminals will autocomplete and list the available rules.
- Any commands that run on your command line can be used, but commands like `rm` will only run on operating systems that have that command.
- You can set easy-to-change variables like compilers to use, or directories to look for headers in. These will substitute as text elsewhere in your Makefile.
- Rules can call other rules.

Efficient Builds

To have the Makefile speed up builds you can add a dependency rule so that unchanged files are not recompiled. This is not necessary for small projects, and I don't always do this for larger projects because I like to maintain full builds that take less than 5 seconds, which is great for iteration time.

```
CC=gcc
INCLUDES=two.h


all: main.o two.o
        $(CC) -o my_program main.o two.o -lm


.PHONY : clean
clean:
        rm -f *.o my_program
```

73

```
%.o: %.c $(INCLUDES)
        $(CC) -c -o $@ $<
```

- `all: main.o two.o` - Indicate that these two files must be built first before executing the command.
- `$(CC) -o my_program main.o two.o -lm` - We use the two `.o` object files rather than `.c` source files. This allows us to split the build into parts.
- `.PHONY : clean` - Prevents make from being confused with a file of the same name, in this case `clean`.
- `rm -f *.o my_program` - Also removes the object files.
- `%.o:` - Give make a rule for creating `.o` files.
- `%.o: %.c $(INCLUDES)` - Rebuild the code if the `.c` or any header in the list changed.
- `$(CC) -c -o $@ $<` - Command to output a `.o` from the `.c` of the same name.

Meta-Build Systems

In the Unix world, you'll come across various tools that are used to create Makefiles configured to a user's system. The *Autotools* - GNU Automake with GNU Autoconf are commonly used. To build those projects you run a configuration script, then run `make`.

```
./configure
make
make install
```

Kitware's CMake https://cmake.org/ meta-build tool is commonly used to distribute large libraries and frameworks. It has the advantage that it can build Visual Studio solution files as well as Makefiles, which is appealing for distributing source code for tools or libraries to a wide audience. After installing CMake you typically create a folder for it to write the build files into, then run

CMake, pointing it at the main folder that contains a `CMakeLists.txt` file. E.g. On a Linux machine, from the directory containing `CMakeLists.txt` I would type:

```
mkdir build
cd build
cmake ..
cmake --build .
```

Where the `cmake --build` command will run the appropriate build command for depending on the generator it used on your platform - `make`, `msbuild`, `xcodebuild`, etc.

CMake requires a `CMakeLists.txt` file in the project, where you create a list of source files, dependencies, and other build settings. Larger projects get very complex, with nested `CMakeLists.txt` files within subdirectories too. It can be quite tricky to keep track of options and settings between these files.

There is also a GUI (graphical user interface) for building with CMake. Some IDEs, such as CLion, and newer versions of Visual Studio, can integrate CMake into the IDE as a project build system.

It is worth your time to familiarise yourself using at least the CMake GUI to build a third-party library for your project to link against. For example, find an interesting library on GitHub to use in your project. If you open CMake GUI and point it at the library's folder containing `CMakeLists.txt` it will ask you what build system you want as output - on Windows that may be a solution for a particular version of Visual Studio, on Unix systems it's probably a Makefile. You can then load the solution and build it from within Visual Studio, or call `make`, from wherever you specify the output directory.

When you are distributing a reasonably complex library project with source code it is worth considering CMake or another meta-build system to give users more flexibility for building it. The function syntax and general advice varies between versions of CMake, so you must first decide which version of CMake to use. You can start with a simple example from https://cmake.org/examples and then follow the extensive developer documentation from Kitware's CMake Wiki https://gitlab.kitware.com/cmake/community/-/wikis/home.

Tips and Common Problems

- Don't get carried away with complicated build systems! It's easy to spend far too much time maintaining these things, and that isn't productive coding.
- It's worth learning how to use and write simple Makefiles, and build from CMake files, because they are so commonly used.
- Using meta-build systems as your main build system will slow down your first-time builds on a machine considerably because they add additional build steps, such as searching for required libraries.
- Using a generated Makefile on subsequent builds will typically still build more slowly than your hand-written Makefile or build script.
- Generated build files can be very difficult to understand and hand-tweak.
- There are a huge variety of build system tools available for C and C++. There is a tool similar to Make, called *Ninja*, that is intended to work with meta-build systems. The Qt project has its own build systems; *qmake* and *Qbs*.
- If you use Visual Studio you can run all its build tools from the command line. They will be on the path if you run the Developer Command Prompt. You may then compile from the command line using `cl.exe`, in a very similar way to GCC and Clang. See Microsoft's online MSVC documentation for command line flags. This can be simpler than setting up project builds in the IDE menus.

```
cl main.c
```

- Try to build new software doing full rebuilds of all your project files on every compile - keeping builds to a few seconds will train you to recognise problematic code. *"I'm not slacking off, my code is compiling!"* is probably a good indication that your build or implementation complexity is far too high, which is impacting your productivity (and the environment and the power bill).

- If your code builds very quickly it is also possible to split a large chunk out into a dynamic/shared library and have your changes recompile and live reload any changes to the code, as you type it, while the main program is still running. This is called **hot reloading** code. You can approach the iteration speed of a scripting language with this approach. Functions for reloading shared object libraries differ between operating systems.
- More complex build systems allow you to support multiple build tools and IDE solutions but tend to slow down your build time and iteration time, and require users to install and learn the build tools.
- Your project's build-for-release should only require **one command or button click**. Multi-step builds invite errors, major goofs, and stress in production.
- Try to keep your build complexity as low as possible - remove unnecessary libraries, files, and headers when a simple function can replace them. Faster build times speed up your iteration time and reduce your development opportunity cost considerably.
- Stick with the simplest-level of tech until you need more. C projects typically build very quickly. Linking libraries adds time. C++ projects typically take longer to build. Templated code or libraries can add considerable build time.
- If your builds are very slow, you can use a tool called **ccache** https://ccache.dev/ to speed up recompiles. My team on one job managed to reduce a 20 minute build down to a few minutes on one large legacy project using this.
- Build systems can be very time-consuming and frustrating to maintain across large multi-team projects using different versions of build tools.

7 End Code Style Arguments with clang-format

How to use clang-format

Clang-format automatically formats your code to a given layout style. Each project usually decides on a code style, and then anyone working on it can apply that style without worrying about it whilst typing.

Programmers can have the strongest of opinions about the least important things. If you really like writing in your own style you can, and have `clang-format` convert your code to the project's style later, perhaps automatically called when you submit your work.

```
clang-format -style=llvm -i *.c
```

The above command will format all your .c files with the LLVM style. Clang-format has a few built-in styles to choose from. You can also customise your own style based on one of those by creating a `.clang-format` file.

Making a `.clang-format` File

To start creating a config file for your project, based on the WebKit style:

```
clang-format -style=webkit -dump-config > .clang-format
```

There's also a pretty neat website to interactively design a format file at https://clangformat.com/.

You can edit the file in a text editor.

- On Unix-derived systems the dot at the start of a filename makes it a "hidden" file, so you may not see it right away with `ls`. You can use `ll` or `ls -lah` so include hidden files and directories in the output.
- Set your favourite style preferences.
- Team members can submit modifications to the project style file.

Using `clang-format` in IDEs

- Put your `.clang-format` file in your project's root directory and it should be automatically found by Visual Studio, Visual Studio Code, or CLion.
- You can use keyboard shortcuts to apply formatting to the whole file, or a selection.
- Other IDEs can have custom keyboard shortcuts set up to call `clang-format` from within the IDE for the current source file.

8 Remove Lint with Static Analysis of Code

Static analysis means analysing your code without running it. A static analysis tool, or **linter** is usually just a compiler that is re-written to provide more information - at the expense of longer error-check time. Lint was a program on Unix in 1978, named after a lint (clothing fluff) remover. It was based on a C compiler.

- Run as part of your build script with a cost in build time, or just occasionally.
- Look up the types of errors they can catch in the manual/website.
- Can hook up to a Continuous Integration system as part of code and compile checks.
- Some IDEs have one built in.
- A good approach is to use more than one linter on your code to get as many potential issues flagged as possible.

Why Use a Linter

Analyse your code without executing it and look for things compiler misses:

- Accessing an array out of bounds.
- Invalid memory access (some types).
- Division by zero.
- Integer overflows.
- Warn about other code likely to cause a bug.
- Help find problems that result in "*But it worked on my computer!*" such as use of uninitialised memory, where existing values in memory may differ.
- Can catch the dread **Heisenbug** that goes away when you look for it (usually it's one of the above problems).
- Static analysis tools can be configured to check if code **conforms to a standard** such as those from Google, MISRA, or NASA's Jet Propulsion Laboratory.

Scan-Build

Scan-build sneakily replaces your compiler with its own stand-in Clang compiler that looks for various problems in your code.

- Is part of the LLVM project
  (https://clang-analyzer.llvm.org/scan-build.html)
- It's a Perl script, so on Windows you need to install Perl first.
- scan-build takes your regular build command as an argument.

If I build the following program with GCC it doesn't complain.

```c
#include <stdio.h>

int main() {
        int array[3] = { 10, 11, 12 };
        printf( "array[4] = %i\n", array[4] );
        return 0;
}
```

We can have scan-build comb over it to help find the mistake.

```
$ scan-build gcc main.c
scan-build: Using '/usr/lib/llvm-8/bin/clang' for static
analysis
main.c:5:2: warning: 2nd function call argument is an
uninitialized value
        printf( "array[4] = %i\n", array[4] );
        ^~~~~~~~~~~~~~~~~~~~~~~~~~~~~~~~~~~~~~~~~~~~~~~~
1 warning generated.
scan-build: 1 bug found.
scan-build: Run 'scan-view
```

`/tmp/scan-build-2019-09-12-154652-2274-1'` to examine bug
reports.

If you supply the `-V` argument to scan-build, or navigate to the directory it gives at the end of the output, you can view the report of bugs in a web browser.

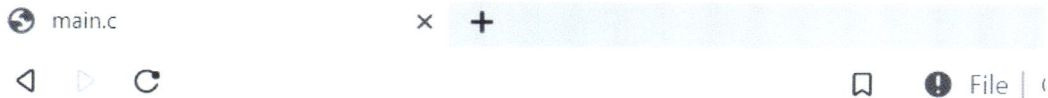

Figure 8.1. Scan-view can output a report for interactive web-browser viewing.

For Xcode users, you don't need to use the command line - the Clang Static Analyzer is integrated directly into the IDE, and has very rich inline *breadcrumb trail* visualisation of problems in the code. See https://clang-analyzer.llvm.org/.

Cppcheck

Cppcheck https://github.com/danmar/cppcheck is free software by Daniel Marjamäki, and provides a very quick GUI tool to analyse your code.

- Performs static analysis on C and C++, including some template support.
- Has a GUI as well as the command-line tool.
- Also in most repositories (`apt-get`, Homebrew, etc).
- Run `cppcheck` on a source code file, or on a directory.

```
$ cppcheck main.c
Checking main.c ...
[main.c:5]: (error) Array 'array[3]' accessed at index 4, which
is out of bounds.
$
```

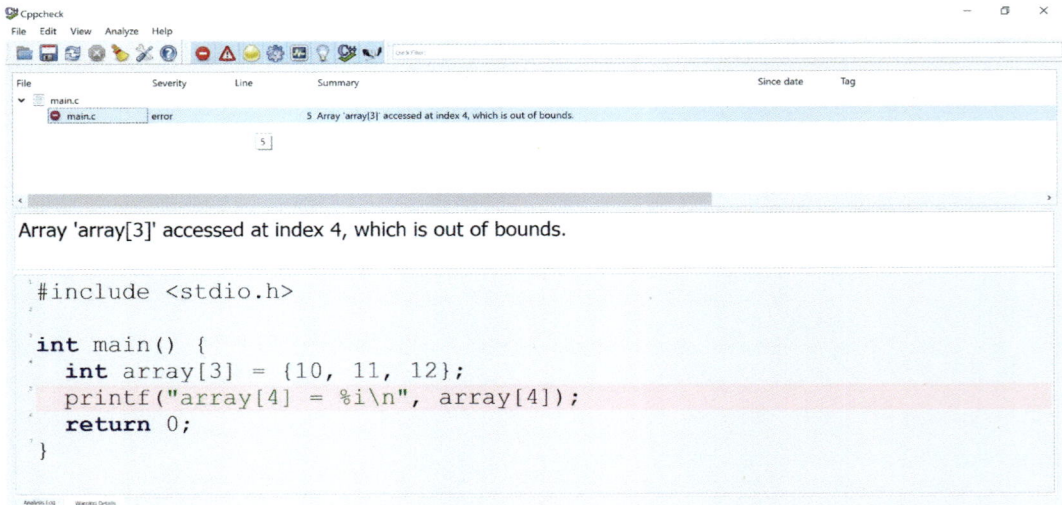

Figure 8.2. Cppcheck also provides an interactive GUI program to help highlight problems in your code.

Clang-Tidy

Clang-tidy (https://clang.llvm.org/extra/clang-tidy/) is another very good linter from the LLVM project. It can also be used to check if **code style** conforms to particular guidelines. It's integrated into some IDEs to provide in-source warnings and errors to lines that it finds break its set of rules.

```
$ clang-tidy my_src/* -- -Imy_include/ -DMY_DEFINES > tidy_output.txt
```

It can produce a lot of output, so it is helpful to redirect that to a file.

$ clang-tidy my_src/* -- -Imy_include/ -DMY_DEFINES > tidy_output.txt

It's possible to feed a single file to clang-tidy or give it a full path to read recursively.

We can give it our headers folders so that it can find files included in our source code.

Clang-tidy will find typical linter problems.

- Dead code and unused variables that you can remove.
- Code where a division by zero is possible.
- Insecure strings copies that can be replaced by size-bounded equivalents.
- Use of uninitialised arguments to functions.
- Logic branches and loops with bad assumptions - "*bath paths*".
- Use of unknown type names (I often write **export** instead of the correct C keyword **extern**).

- Use of bug-prone code constructs.
- Clang-tidy often finds problems that the other linters do not.

Clang-tidy can also check code against a set of conformance standards, specified with the -checks= argument. An optional dash before a checks option removes a set of checks. Your team may decide to use the Google coding conventions. The following command removes all default checks, and adds all the Google checks:

```
clang-tidy -checks=-*,google-* my_src/* -- -Imy_include/
```

9 Fuzz Testing with AFL

```
 Terminal - anton@the_technodrome: ~/projects/antons_howto_guides/book_testi  ⬆ _ ▫ ✕
 File   Edit   View   Terminal   Tabs   Help

                    american fuzzy lop 2.52b (test_ppm_fuzz)
   ┌─ process timing ──────────────────────┐┌─ overall results ─────┐
   │        run time : 0 days, 0 hrs, 10 min, 53 sec ││ cycles done : 2      │
   │   last new path : 0 days, 0 hrs, 10 min, 48 sec ││ total paths : 17     │
   │ last uniq crash : none seen yet        ││ uniq crashes : 0     │
   │  last uniq hang : none seen yet        ││  uniq hangs : 0      │
   ├─ cycle progress ──────────┬─ map coverage ──────────┤
   │  now processing : 5* (29.41%)    │    map density : 0.04% / 0.05%    │
   │ paths timed out : 0 (0.00%)      │ count coverage : 1.24 bits/tuple  │
   ├─ stage progress ──────────┼─ findings in depth ─────┤
   │    now trying : bitflip 1/1         │ favored paths : 7 (41.18%)       │
   │   stage execs : 391k/3.84M (10.18%) │  new edges on : 7 (41.18%)       │
   │   total execs : 453k                │ total crashes : 0 (0 unique)     │
   │   exec speed : 621.1/sec            │  total tmouts : 0 (0 unique)     │
   ├─ fuzzing strategy yields ──────────┴─ path geometry ─────────┤
   │   bit flips : 3/2840, 0/2830, 0/2810      │    levels : 4        │
   │  byte flips : 0/355, 0/162, 0/146         │   pending : 7        │
   │  arithmetics : 3/9542, 0/5525, 0/1898     │  pend fav : 0        │
   │   known ints : 0/726, 0/3522, 0/5599      │ own finds : 11       │
   │   dictionary : 0/0, 0/0, 0/287            │  imported : n/a      │
   │        havoc : 5/23.6k, 0/832             │ stability : 100.00%  │
   │         trim : 0.04%/2025, 46.94%         │                      │
   └───────────────────────────────┘      [cpu000: 26%]
```

Figure 9.1. American Fuzzy Lop fuzzing my PPM reader/writer code based on a set of sample input images to read. It builds a folder of crash reproduction cases.

Fuzz Testing and Why You Should Use It

Fuzz testing is an automated testing process of hardening or bullet-proofing your code to validate and handle invalid inputs gracefully. It is most useful with languages that are not memory safe such as C and C++, which are prone to programmer errors.

Fuzz testing uses a program called a **fuzzer** that generates randomised variations of input data and throws them at your code, and reports every unique crash it manages to cause. Note that it will also report an assertion triggering as a crash - so if you're using assertions to report bad inputs to a user then you'll need to handle those cases gracefully instead.

We use fuzz testing to catch any unhandled or unexpected **edge cases**. Doing this with real testers is laborious and error-prone. Some fuzzers use a genetic algorithm to create generations of valid-looking inputs that explore deeper into the paths of your program. This also gives fuzz testing a value for **security-hardening** your code against deliberately malicious inputs.

How to Use a Fuzzer

The general process is:

1. Build the functions you want to test into a little program, where the inputs can be represented by a file.

```c
#include "my_ppm_stuff.h" // the header for my image functions
#include <stdint.h>
#include <stdio.h>
#include <stdlib.h>
#include <string.h>

int main( int argc, char** argv ) {
  const char* file_in  = "in.ppm";
```

```
  const char* file_out = "out.ppm";
  if (argc > 1) { file_in = argv[1]; }
  if (argc > 2) { file_out = argv[2]; }

  // i want to test this function that reads an image
  struct image_t my_image = ppm_read( file_in );
  if ( !my_image.ptr ) {
    fprintf( stderr, "ERROR: could not read image `%s`\n", file_in );
    return 1;
  }

  // and i'll secondarily make sure the writer works afterwards
  bool success = ppm_write( file_out, my_image );
  if ( !success ) {
    fprintf( stderr, "ERROR: could not write image `%s`\n", file_out );
    return 1;
  }

  free( my_image.ptr );
  return 0;
}
```

2. Give a fuzzer a folder of *small* valid sample input files.
   For example, we could create some small test images, that are still big
   enough to create several randomised variations on. I made a set of 8x8
   pixel alien invaders, and a few in different sizes and colours.

```
fuzzer_inputs/8x8invader0.ppm
fuzzer_inputs/8x8invader1.ppm
fuzzer_inputs/8x8invader2.ppm
...
fuzzer_inputs/16x16letter_a.ppm
...
```

3. Install the American Fuzzy Lop (AFL) fuzzer. Website: http://lcamtuf.coredump.cx/afl/ or on Google's GitHub https://github.com/google/AFL.
On Ubuntu you can install from the repositories:

```
sudo apt-get install afl
```

4. Use afl-gcc or afl-clang to build a *clean* compile of your program (e.g. `make clean && make all`) in place of gcc or clang. It probably helps to give your fuzzer build a different file name to the regular build:

```
afl-gcc -g -o test_ppm_fuzz main.c my_ppm_stuff.c -I ./
```

5. Run your program with afl-fuzz:

```
afl-fuzz -i fuzzer_inputs/ -o fuzzer_outputs/ --
./test_ppm_fuzz @@
```

The fuzzer will look for sample input files in the directory we made, and make a new directory called `fuzzer_outputs/` where it will put any input files it generates that cause your program to crash. The `--` separator separates the fuzzer and its arguments from your program and its arguments.

If you normally run your program with the file name as an argument (we do in our example code) as e.g. `./test_ppm the_test_file.ppm` then `afl_fuzz` will feed it the correct file name where the `@@` appears in the command above. Any additional command-line arguments you need to send to your program go at the end.

AFL will probably warn about a few system settings. If you don't want to address as per instructions then you can suppress them. Put the following all on one line.

```
AFL_EXIT_WHEN_DONE=1 AFL_I_DONT_CARE_ABOUT_MISSING_CRASHES=1
AFL_SKIP_CPUFREQ=1 afl-fuzz -i fuzzer_inputs/ -o
fuzzer_outputs/ -- ./test_ppm_fuzz @@
```

6. Either wait for the entire fuzzing process to finish (it can take an extremely long time), or after a couple of hours, have a look in the `fuzzer_outputs/crashes/` directory for anything it puts in there while it's running. You can also halt the fuzzer with `CTRL+C`. Then you can run your regular program with these as input files to reproduce the crashes that were found.

```
./test_ppm fuzzer_outputs/crashes/id:00000_very_long_filename
```

For example, my first crashing input file was named

```
id:000000,sig:06,src:000001,op:flip1,pos:0
```

If you run this in an interactive debugger, or e.g. get a backtrace after a crash from GDB, then you can find where your program is crashing pretty quickly. Try to fix all the problems highlighted by the crash reproductions. Some of these will be false positives or duplicates of the same issue, although AFL does a good job of minimising those. Can you guess what's next?

7. Run the fuzzing process again. Repeat the process until no further bugs are found.

For an example to fuzz that definitely has a problem, you can add a deliberate crash to your PPM image reader code. The samples still have to load, but random variations will have invalid data. You can put an `assert()` if the "P6" number at the start of the file wasn't there. The samples will have a valid P6, but random inputs may not. The idea here is to find places like this that crash, and fix your code so that it gracefully exits or continues when malformed inputs are found.

```
char type[2];
int n = fscanf( fptr, "%c%c\n", &type[0], &type[1] );
if ( n != 2 || type[0] != 'P' || type[1] != '6' ) {
  assert( false ); /***** deliberate crash for the fuzzer to find
and can be easily fixed ******/
```

In the fuzzer_outputs/ directory, AFL creates a lot of content.

- `queue/` - AFL builds a set of test inputs here from your samples.
- `crashes/` - inputs that caused unique crashes are stored here.
- `hangs/` - inputs that caused the test program to time out are stored here.

Tips and Common Problems

- Security developers, hackers, and testers are usually GNU/Linux based so you'll find limited support for these kinds of tools on macOS, and barely any on Windows. You could try the WinAFL fork of AFL on Windows: https://n0where.net/fuzzing-windows-binaries-winafl.
- Be careful fuzzing on a solid-state disk. Fuzzers can do a lot of disk writes, which may wear on the drive.
- If your program has custom intercepts for `SIGSEGV` or `SIGABRT` (e.g. to write a backtrace on crash) this can interfere with the fuzzer's crash detection. Disable during fuzzing.
- Also build your program with address sanitiser (ASan) to get more useful output from the fuzzer.
- If you are reproducing a crash don't forget to build your regular program with debug symbols to get a sensible backtrace.
- AFL can also be set up to generate data for a program that reads from `stdin` instead of files. It can also test networks.
- Fuzzing (and other automated testing) can also be used to test GUI interactions, mouse clicks, and anything else you desire, although you may have to code fuzzer hooks yourself for special input cases.
- The community-supported AFL++ project has various performance and CPU usage improvements and can also be found on GitHub:

https://github.com/vanhauser-thc/AFLplusplus. At the time of writing it also includes a script for getting past CPU governor and kernel core pattern issues you may see reported by AFL under `AFLplusplus/afl-system-config`.

- The `docs/` folder of AFL contains tips for fuzzing more quickly, enabling multi-core fuzzing, and descriptions of various errors, reported in the UI in red text.

10 Asm Inspection

Assembly code (asm) is the **low-level language** in your compiler chain, one level before the assembler converts it into the CPU's native machine code. You usually never see it when you compile your code. It's worth looking at because C and C++ are **high-level languages** that can give an imprecise picture of how your code translates to machine instructions. Each C instruction usually translates to a few asm instructions. One asm instruction usually translates to one machine code instruction. Assembly for modern CPUs is 64-bit **x86-64**, often referred to as **x64**.

Why Inspecting Asm is Useful

Ever run a debug build of your program and it's very sluggish compared to a release build? This usually indicates the compiler has to do a lot of additional optimisation work on your code to get it to run properly, or that it has lots of extra debugging checks built in. This is a really common complaint of C++ programmers, and you see people not testing with debug builds as a consequence, which means they lose useful information. It's usually hard to see the difference between builds when we are looking at our C or C++ code. We can get some insight by comparing the assembled code (asm) of the debug and optimised builds.

Do you need to learn how to code in asm directly? No, not for most jobs any more, but it's still insightful to get a feel for how code relates to instructions in asm - much closer to the compiled machine code that will actually be processed. Making a habit of inspecting and comparing code, with just a small amount of looking up what the different asm instructions do, will give you a perspective on code complexity that most programmers don't have.

- Learn some fundamental asm instructions.
- Reason about how much your code is optimised by the compiler. Find out what was optimised out.
- Find out how "heavy" convenient abstractions or library code really is.
- Compare the relative complexity of alternative functions or data structures.

- Gain a clearer intuition of what compilers do when they optimise, and where you need to take care.

If you have a better understanding of the relative instruction complexity of different code abstractions you can help:

- Improve the performance of your team's codebase.
- Reduce the disk size of your compiled programs.
- Make more informed decisions about choices of data structure and algorithm abstractions.
- Understand what different compiler optimisation flags do to the code, and how much additional work this might add during compilation.
- Debug exceptionally tricky problems into the asm instruction level.

Assembly Concepts Overview

Assembly instructions are made up of two parts

1. 3-4 letter **opcode** for a particular operation.
2. The names of up to 2 **registers** or memory addresses, containing values that are operated on.

The asm for an instruction to add two integers may look like

```
add eax, edx
```

Where

- add is the opcode for adding two integers.
- eax is the name of the first register.
- edx is the name of the second register.
- The result overwrites the first register.

In asm for x86-64 CPU architectures, there are a set of general purpose 64-bit registers that can be used by name. It's also possible to use half of a register by using its equivalent 32-bit name.

x86-64 General Purpose Registers

64-bit name	rax	rbx	rcx	rdx	rsi	rdi	rbp	rsp	r8	r9	...	r15
32-bit name	eax	ebx	ecx	edx	esi	edi	ebp	esp	r8d	r9d	...	r15d

There are also a set of floating point registers `xmm0-xmm15`. We can see that `eax` and `edx` registers are 32-bits - the size of an `int`, and we will see these in the asm of programs where we add two integers.

Compiler Assembly Output

You can ask your compiler to output the asm from a C file. In GCC you supply the `-S` flag.

```
gcc -S my_file.c
```

This will generate a file with the `.s` extension, which you can open in a text editor. You will see the asm under labels for each of your functions. You will also see any constants such as strings.

Most debuggers also let you step through assembly code, which can be quite a useful live view of asm. These tools are sometimes useful, but a bit overwhelming if you haven't learned the basic concepts of asm yet.

Compiler Explorer is a much more convenient tool for asm inspection, and for learning about asm.

Compiler Explorer

Started by Matt Godbolt, Compiler Explorer (https://godbolt.org/) was originally used for understanding the compiled complexity of different C++ constructs. It is a website-based tool for **interactive** asm inspection and comparison.

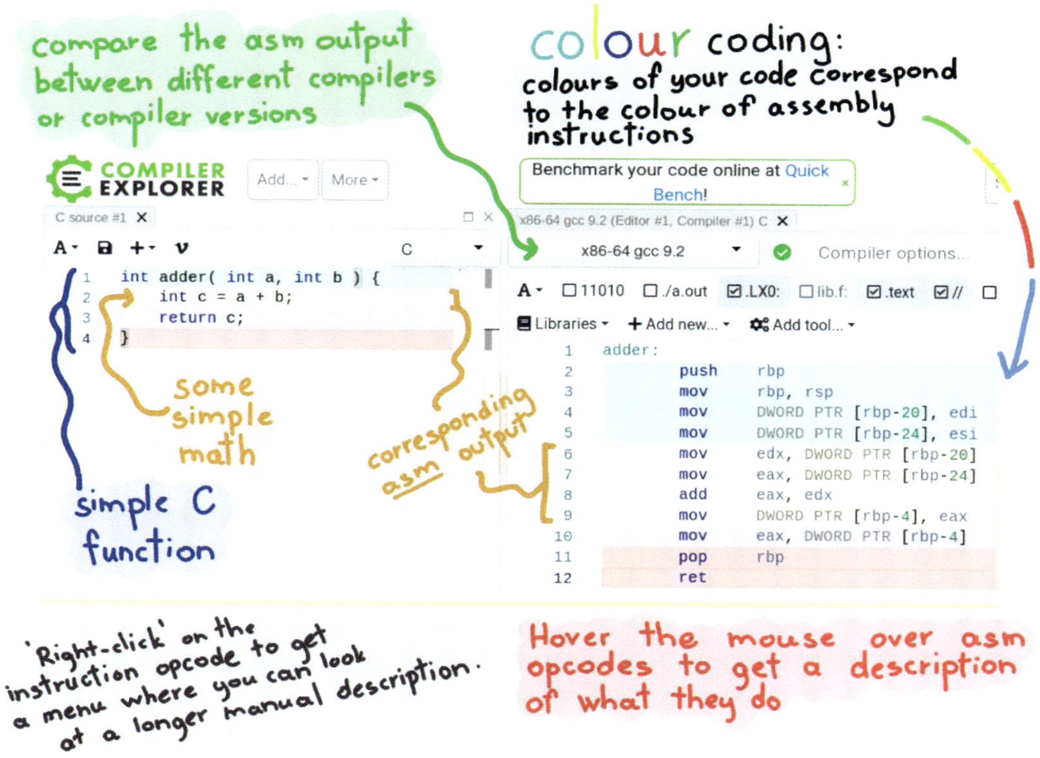

compare the asm output between different compilers or compiler versions

colour coding: colours of your code correspond to the colour of assembly instructions

some simple math

simple C function

corresponding asm output

'Right-click' on the instruction opcode to get a menu where you can look at a longer manual description.

Hover the mouse over asm opcodes to get a description of what they do

Figure 10.1. The Compiler Explorer website. I wrote a simple C function in the left panel. Line 2 has some simple maths, coloured yellow. The corresponding asm output for it is also shown in yellow in the right-hand panel.

Compiler Explorer is Open Source, and on GitHub https://github.com/mattgodbolt/compiler-explorer.

How to Use Compiler Explorer

1. Choose a compiler, and a version of compiler, in the drop-down in the right.
2. Paste a small, stand-alone snippet of your code into the panel on the left, or load one of the examples from the load/save menu.
3. There is limited support for libraries, but including standard libraries is fine.
4. The right-hand side will assemble your code, and show you different sections by colour. You can hover over your code sections to highlight the corresponding asm.
5. In the compiler options text input, you can add optimisation flags such as -O3.
6. You can add multiple output panels, which lets you side-by-side compare optimisation levels and compilers.
7. An additional panel allows you to compile and interactively **execute** your code on different compilers as well.

I wrote a very simple function into Compiler Explorer's C source area. You can try writing this, or a similar function, and inspect the asm generated.

```
int adder( int a, int b ) {
    int c = a + b;
    return c;
}
```

- Note that the generated asm does not show our **variable names**, and we need to hunt through, following the register names to trace what is happening to our variables.
- Opcodes have names push mov add pop ret. If you **hover the mouse** over the opcodes in Compiler Explorer you can get a description of what they do, and what the arguments to each mean. This is a great way to learn asm! You can probably guess what add and ret do!
- Enter optimisation level -O3 in the compiler options input field. What

happens to the asm?
- Try switching to different compilers and versions in the dropdown menu. Is the output the same at different optimisation levels? You could try one of your own functions here.

With Compiler Explorer we have a sandbox code palette to try some more simple functions. A little bit of tinkering in Compiler Explorer can help you learn some asm, and how it relates to your original code. You can take this knowledge to improve your debugging - now stepping into the asm is a little more useful!

Recommended Reading

To supplement your experimentation in Compiler Explorer, let me suggest the following resources to learn more about x86-64 compiler assembly.

1. *x86-64 An Overview* - slides from Andrew Moss' *Compilation Technologies* university course. https://mechani.se/comp/09/index.html
2. Matt Godbolt's Compiler Explorer walkthrough videos on YouTube. https://www.youtube.com/user/mattatgodboltorg/
3. *Introduction to x64 Assembly* by Chris Lomont on Intel Developer Zone (March 2012) https://software.intel.com/en-us/articles/introduction-to-x64-assembly
4. *Modern X86 Assembly Language Programming* by Daniel Kusswurm, Apress; 2nd ed. edition (Dec. 2018), ISBN-13: 978-1484240625.

Tips and Common Problems

- I suggest using Compiler Explorer to test one small function or data structure in isolation. I wouldn't try pasting in a large graphical program and expect it to work.
- It used to be common to mix asm into C code to hand-optimise sections. You can still do this in GCC and Clang, but Microsoft removed this capability from Visual Studio. There is a newer equivalent called **intrinsics**, which is supported on the most popular 64-bit compilers, and also provides some highly optimised, small, function-like operations.
- Comparing the complexity of functions and data types from the standard libraries is where asm inspection is most useful as an additional complexity measurement of code.
- Fewer asm instructions does not necessarily result in faster programs. The highest compiler optimisation level can produce much longer, faster asm code.
- Asm inspection gets really interesting when comparing the complexity of abstract data types in C++, which has much more complex container types than C. Try substituting an `std::vector` with an array, and comparing the asm. Then try again at a higher compiler optimisation level. How much work is moved from run-time complexity to compile-time complexity when we increase compiler optimisations?

11 Memory Debuggers, Sanitisers, and Cache Simulators

In C and C++ it's easy to make mistakes misusing memory. Some of these issues can be found with static analysis tools and fuzzing, but other issues depend on the path taken by the program during run-time. Typical problems that occur at run time relate to dynamic memory allocation, deallocation, and access. Common memory issues include:

- **Memory leaks** - allocating memory without freeing it. This can compound if done in a main program loop.
- Double free of memory.
- Accessing memory after freeing it.
- Accessing memory outside of an allocated block.
- Using uninitialised pointers.
- Relying on **undefined behaviour** in the language, that compilers may change to perform optimisations.

Consider the following buggy C code, which compiles and runs without error:

```c
#include <stdlib.h>

void my_func() {
        int* x = malloc( 16 * sizeof( int ) );
        x[16] = 0; // out of bounds of memory ( heap overrun )
        // memory is not freed
}

int main() {
        my_func();
        return 0;
}
```

Other languages use more sophisticated memory models with **garbage collection** and **bounds checking**, to mitigate most of these problems, at the cost of performance and compilation time. It's possible to use or write more sophisticated C and C++ data structures to get some of these features, if we want them.

We can use a variety of stand-alone and built-in tools to check our program's memory usage for invalid operations and **leaks**.

Valgrind Memcheck   Valgrind CacheGrind   UBSan   ASan

Valgrind Memcheck

Valgrind's memcheck is a command-line memory debugging tool for Linux that can help you find memory leaks in your running program.

If we compile our leaky program sample, above, with debugging symbols, we can run it with Valgrind's leak checker.

```
gcc leaky.c -g
valgrind --leak-check=yes ./my_program
```

- If your program has command-line arguments, you can add them after the binary's name: ./my_program arg1 arg2
- If you don't see file and line numbers in your output from Valgrind, compile your program with debug symbols, and try again.
- Valgrind will report an invalid write of a 4-byte integer on line 5, where x[16] = 0;. The memory allocated was only 16 integers long - indices 0-15 are valid.
- Valgrind will report a leak of 64 bytes (the 16 4-byte integers we allocated).
- Your code may be fine, but Valgrind can also find leaks and other memory issues in libraries, drivers, and other code that you have relied on. This may be from your misuse of the library's API - read the instructions again!
- Technically, we don't need to free the allocated memory in our example program, since it is released at program exit.
- If we were to call our allocating function within a loop, or in response to a user input, it might create an unmanageable leak.

```
Terminal - anton@the_technodrome: ~/projects/howto_guides_pvt/book_testing/11_valgrind

File  Edit  View  Terminal  Tabs  Help

anton:~/projects/howto_guides_pvt/book_testing/11_valgrind[master]$ gcc main.c -g
anton:~/projects/howto_guides_pvt/book_testing/11_valgrind[master]$ valgrind --leak-check=yes ./my_pro
gram
==30065== Memcheck, a memory error detector
==30065== Copyright (C) 2002-2017, and GNU GPL'd, by Julian Seward et al.
==30065== Using Valgrind-3.13.0 and LibVEX; rerun with -h for copyright info
==30065== Command: ./my_program
==30065==
==30065== Invalid write of size 4
==30065==    at 0x108668: my_func (main.c:17)
==30065==    by 0x10867E: main (main.c:22)
==30065==  Address 0x522d080 is 0 bytes after a block of size 64 alloc'd
==30065==    at 0x4C2FB0F: malloc (in /usr/lib/valgrind/vgpreload_memcheck-amd64-linux.so)
==30065==    by 0x10865B: my_func (main.c:16)
==30065==    by 0x10867E: main (main.c:22)
==30065==
==30065==
==30065== HEAP SUMMARY:
==30065==      in use at exit: 64 bytes in 1 blocks
==30065==    total heap usage: 1 allocs, 0 frees, 64 bytes allocated
==30065==
==30065== 64 bytes in 1 blocks are definitely lost in loss record 1 of 1
==30065==    at 0x4C2FB0F: malloc (in /usr/lib/valgrind/vgpreload_memcheck-amd64-linux.so)
==30065==    by 0x10865B: my_func (main.c:16)
==30065==    by 0x10867E: main (main.c:22)
==30065==
==30065== LEAK SUMMARY:
==30065==    definitely lost: 64 bytes in 1 blocks
==30065==    indirectly lost: 0 bytes in 0 blocks
==30065==      possibly lost: 0 bytes in 0 blocks
==30065==    still reachable: 0 bytes in 0 blocks
==30065==         suppressed: 0 bytes in 0 blocks
==30065==
==30065== For counts of detected and suppressed errors, rerun with: -v
==30065== ERROR SUMMARY: 2 errors from 2 contexts (suppressed: 0 from 0)
anton:~/projects/howto_guides_pvt/book_testing/11_valgrind[master]$
```

Figure 11.1. Valgrind's leak check found both the out-of-bounds memory access, and that we didn't free the allocated heap memory.

Valgrind is very powerful, but is primarily a Linux tool, and makes your program run very slowly, so doesn't suit every program. On one job, the embedded device we were working on had a process watchdog that would kill Valgrind before it finished because it used too many system resources.

Be warned - Valgrind can not inspect the equivalent bounds and allocation errors that occur in dynamically allocated **stack memory**.

103

ASan - Address Sanitizer

ASan is Address Sanitizer, a Clang tool that you can add to your program's build to help you debug memory issues in your running program. ASan can be used in command-line builds with Clang, is integrated with other sanitiser tools in Xcode through checkboxes in the *Scheme→Diagnostics* panel, and at the time of writing ASan is also being integrated into new versions of Visual Studio. It covers much of the same memory error checking surface as Valgrind, but it's faster and has some limited support outside of Linux. It's partially built into your program (instrumented), but also uses an external ASan library that requires Clang for linking.

```
clang -fsanitize=address -g leaky.c -o ./my_program
./my_program
```

Running the program will give us the same errors caught as Valgrind, and with more detailed information.

```
SUMMARY: AddressSanitizer: heap-buffer-overflow (/home/anton/projects/howto_guides_pvt/book_testing/11
_valgrind/my_program+0x51213e)
Shadow bytes around the buggy address:
  0x0c0c7fff7fb0: 00 00 00 00 00 00 00 00 00 00 00 00 00 00 00 00
  0x0c0c7fff7fc0: 00 00 00 00 00 00 00 00 00 00 00 00 00 00 00 00
  0x0c0c7fff7fd0: 00 00 00 00 00 00 00 00 00 00 00 00 00 00 00 00
  0x0c0c7fff7fe0: 00 00 00 00 00 00 00 00 00 00 00 00 00 00 00 00
  0x0c0c7fff7ff0: 00 00 00 00 00 00 00 00 00 00 00 00 00 00 00 00
=>0x0c0c7fff8000: fa fa fa fa 00 00 00 00 00 00 00 00[fa]fa fa fa
  0x0c0c7fff8010: fa fa fa fa fa fa fa fa fa fa fa fa fa fa fa fa
  0x0c0c7fff8020: fa fa fa fa fa fa fa fa fa fa fa fa fa fa fa fa
  0x0c0c7fff8030: fa fa fa fa fa fa fa fa fa fa fa fa fa fa fa fa
  0x0c0c7fff8040: fa fa fa fa fa fa fa fa fa fa fa fa fa fa fa fa
  0x0c0c7fff8050: fa fa fa fa fa fa fa fa fa fa fa fa fa fa fa fa
Shadow byte legend (one shadow byte represents 8 application bytes):
  Addressable:           00
  Partially addressable: 01 02 03 04 05 06 07
  Heap left redzone:       fa
```

Figure 11.2. ASan's output about the invalid memory access even visualises the nearby valid and invalid memory locations.

You can compile your program with optimisation flags at `-O1` or higher to get better performance with ASan. ASan will deliberately crash your program after detecting the first error. For development builds it can be handy to always build with ASan, as it's not too slow to work with, and can catch errors before they get built on top of.

To get file, function name, and line information added to the output, you can run your program with llvm-symbolizer (if you have it installed).

```
ASAN_SYMBOLIZER_PATH=/usr/bin/llvm-symbolizer ./my_program
```

- If you do not see line numbers beside error reports, check that you have compiled your program with the debug flag -g.
- If llvm-symbolizer is not on your system check that you have installed the main (meta) llvm package in addition to a specific, numbered, version of llvm.

UBSan - Undefined Behaviour Sanitizer

UBSan is Clang's sanitiser for undefined behaviour. It's a potential weak point in your code if your program works, but relies on the way the compiler **currently** implements behaviour that is **undefined** by the language.

An example of undefined behaviour that has broken older code on newer compilers is **bit shifting** of values in variables. If the shifted bit goes off either end of the variable, what happens? If a negative number is bit-shifted, what happens?

```c
#include <stdio.h>

int main() {
        int b = -1;
        b = b << 1; // shift a negative number
        printf( "b = %i\n", b );

        int c = 1 << 32; // 1 is cast to a 32-bit integer
        printf( "c = %i\n", c );
        return 0;
}
```

UBSan performs extra compile-time checks, but can also use a UBSan library to provide additional checks at run time.

```
clang -fsanitize=undefined main.c
./my_program
```

The compiler sometimes produces a warning for things that are undefined behaviour, but it doesn't catch both of our examples. The run-time UBSan does report both issues.

```
main.c:5:8: runtime error: left shift of negative value -1
b = -2
main.c:8:12: runtime error: shift exponent 32 is too large for
32-bit type 'int'
c = 8959232
```

Valgrind CacheGrind

Cachegrind is a CPU **cache simulator** and **branch prediction** profiler in the Valgrind tools. It can help you estimate the number of **cache misses** incurred by your program. This is one of the most common performance bottlenecks on modern computers. If we can reduce the number of cache misses we can gain significant performance advantage.

The CPU's cache is a set of extremely fast, but expensive, memory buffers that sits close to the CPU - in between registers and RAM. Modern machines have 3-4 cache levels - L1 next to the CPU to L3 or L4 - called LL (last level), before RAM. Accessing data from the cache is about an order of magnitude faster than accessing data from RAM, and faster again than accessing from disk, or over a network.

- When your program accesses data, it will check the first level of fast cache memory for it. If it finds the data we call this a **cache hit**.
- If it does not find the data, it proceeds to the next cache level, and so on, and finally to main memory (RAM). We call this a **cache miss**.
- When data is fetched from an address in RAM, a small chunk of data adjacent in memory (a **cache line**'s size - usually 32, 64, or 128 bytes), is **preemptively** moved with it to the cache.
- A cache miss at L1 costs about 10 CPU cycles.
- A cache miss at LL costs up to 200 CPU cycles.
- Therefore the idea for optimising performance is to minimise cache misses by having as much data as possible already in the cache.

The strategy is generally

1. Collect statistics on the number of cache misses in your program.
2. Modify your program to reduce the number of cache misses (fewer RAM round-trips).
3. Collect statistics again to verify a reduction in cache misses and an improvement in performance.

We can also reduce the number of branching conditions in our code, and change our switch and if-statement clauses to improve the branch prediction performance results. A branch misprediction costs 10-30 cycles.

How to Use CacheGrind

Compile your program with debug symbols, and compiler optimisation turned to your release settings, to give a realistic simulation.

```
gcc -g -O3 main.c
valgrind --tool=cachegrind --branch-sim=yes ./my_program
```

The output from CacheGrind will list 3 sections:

1. Cache accesses for instruction fetches (prefixed by 'I').
2. Cache accesses for data fetches (prefixed by 'D').
3. Combined statistics for both.
4. Branch simulation statistics.

```
==1774== I    refs:        207,674
==1774== I1   misses:        1,097
==1774== LLi  misses:        1,080
==1774== I1   miss rate:      0.53%
==1774== LLi  miss rate:      0.52%
==1774==
==1774== D    refs:         67,889  (51,824 rd   + 16,065 wr)
==1774== D1   misses:         3,134  ( 2,501 rd   +    633 wr)
==1774== LLd  misses:         2,595  ( 2,033 rd   +    562 wr)
==1774== D1   miss rate:        4.6% (    4.8%   +    3.9%  )
==1774== LLd  miss rate:        3.8% (    3.9%   +    3.5%  )
==1774==
==1774== LL refs:            4,231  ( 3,598 rd   +    633 wr)
==1774== LL misses:           3,675  ( 3,113 rd   +    562 wr)
==1774== LL miss rate:          1.3% (    1.2%   +    3.5%  )
==1774==
==1774== Branches:          40,098  (39,311 cond +    787 ind)
```

```
==1774== Mispredicts:      4,785  ( 4,642 cond +      143 ind)
==1774== Mispred rate:     11.9% (  11.8%      +    18.2%   )
```

Some compilers do a better job of optimising your code against branch prediction and cache misses. The Intel C compiler historically has done the best.

If your compiler does not help then you may need to modify your code. Improving the cache hit ratio and branch prediction are generally best done by following up-to-date guides produced by the CPU manufacturer, which typically list things like:

- For branch prediction - rearrange if-statements and switch-statements such that the most likely clauses are given first.
- For cache misses - rearrange nested loops over data such that data access order mirrors data storage order.
- Data accessed together should be stored together in memory.
- Avoid heap and global memory where local function variables will do - they are more likely to be on the stack and in the level 1 cache then.
- For a huge list of very specific up-to-date C and C++ small examples see Agner Fog's *Optimizing software in C++*, from the Technical University of Denmark, last updated in 2019.
  https://www.agner.org/optimize/optimizing_cpp.pdf

After making changes run the program with a timer to see if it's faster, and run the cache simulation again.

Tips and Common Problems

- Try to write your programs such that all errors reported by Valgrind are fixed right away, before adding new features. This will make a significant reliability improvement to your software, and reduce the risk of building onto buggy software, which can be expensive to modify later.
- Valgrind may find errors that never show up during debugging. This doesn't mean they won't show up on an end-user's machine!
- Valgrind builds require 10-30x the normal processor resources. If your program is running too slowly, or Valgrind is not suitable for testing on e.g. an embedded device, then try ASan instead.
- It's possible to add memory leak checks to your code by writing a wrapper around memory allocation and freeing calls. An example of this is `stb_leakcheck` https://github.com/nothings/stb/.
- It's also a valid strategy to allocate all of the memory required by your program at the start, in a large block. It can then all be released at once, or will be automatically when the program exits, without needing to worry about leaks.
- I always make it extremely clear if a C function I have written will allocate memory, and if there is a matching function, at the same level, that the user of my code can call to free it.
- A good C API will allow a programmer to provide their own `malloc()` and `free()` functions to it, so that the library can use the same memory allocation strategy as the rest of the program.
- Remember to disable compiler sanitiser flags before shipping, or your program will depend on the libraries for those tools.
- Address Sanitizer's memory leak checker is only enabled by default on Linux. To enable it on macOS you need to set an environment variable before running your program: `ASAN_OPTIONS=detect_leaks=1`.
- A good example for testing CacheGrind on, where you can see a significant cache miss difference between sequential and random

memory access alternatives can be found at
https://github.com/perfanov/CacheMissExample.
- KCacheGrind is a very useful front-end for CacheGrind that can drill down into more detail to find hotspots in your program for cache misses. It also visualises profiler outputs and call graphs
http://kcachegrind.sourceforge.net/html/Home.html

12 *It worked on my computer!* Shipping the Program

Distributing your compiled C or C++ program such that it actually runs on another computer has a few challenges.

1. It needs to be compiled for the same CPU **architecture** (64-bit or 32-bit) and **operating system** as the user's machine.
2. Any dynamic libraries that it has as **dependencies** must either be installed on the user's machine, or come bundled with the application.
3. It must be able to find and read and write all the **assets** and configuration files it needs. Replace fixed file paths with relative paths!
4. Some operating systems require programs to be in a specific archive or folder structure - an **application bundle**. These sometimes need to be officially approved.
5. You must comply with **copyright** and **licences** of any source code, tools, and assets that your program uses (don't forget this includes typefaces/fonts). This may require reproducing copyright notices, licences, and source code with your application.
6. You should think about presenting some minimum **system requirements**.
7. Create a package, archive, or installer containing all of the required bits that will extract with the correct directory structure.

You can avoid many of these issues if you ship the source code, and have the user compile it, but that has issues to consider too.

1. You must provide clear, concise build and run instructions.
2. The user must have a compatible compiler, and all the external dependencies required by your source code.
3. You need to provide the licence and copyright limitations of your own work, in addition to meeting licence and copyright obligations of any dependencies.
4. You either need to bundle any external dependencies, or distribute your program through a **package manager** system that can pull them in from a repository.

5. Your build system and number of installation and build steps should be simple enough for your target audience to use.

Wrangling Shared Libraries

Shared (dynamically linked) libraries are probably the biggest issue for C and C++ code distribution. Your ideal tactic for distribution and future-proofing your program is to reduce the number of libraries that your program uses. A small dose of *not invented here syndrome* can help with that.

1. Determine all of your release binary's dependencies. *Beware!* Dependencies may also have dependencies, and you should itemise these too.
2. Think about removing libraries from your project that you can replace with small drop-in libraries or by writing the required functions yourself. This protects you from future licence issues, and loss-of-support issues you can't control, as well as simplifying your library distribution problem.
3. Where possible, and within their licence terms, you can compile libraries as static; which removes an external dependency and builds it into your program instead. This also adds size to your binary, and may it take longer to compile your release build. The catch here is if you use another external library that also links to this library - you might get a dependency confusion. This can be problematic for static linking core language libraries like `libc`.
4. There may be some system library dependencies - usually video drivers and core operating system libraries - that you can assume will be available in some compatible form on the user's computer. These are much more likely to be ABI-stable (application binary interface) between versions, and you are unlikely to be allowed to distribute them anyway, so cross these off the list.
5. Everything else needs to be distributed with your program. On Windows the `.exe` will search in its own folder for the DLL files it needs - you should be able to put them all there. To test this you can try to run your program from an empty folder, and add the DLL files one at a time to fix any complaint pop-ups. On Linux and macOS this is not the case, and requires the use of tools and library path changes.
6. The compiler's language run-time libraries used to build your program

also need to be accounted for. On Windows you can distribute the compiler's libraries with your program, bake them into your binary statically, or have your users install the matching **redistributable** package for your compiler version. On Linux, unless you create some installation instructions or script for fetching libraries, you will need to bundle them with your program, ideally using an old version for maximum compatibility across distributions, current and future.

7. For C shared libraries you can have your program open them at run time, using e.g. `dlopen()` or `LoadLibrary()` instead of linking to them. You can handle libraries linked at run time more flexibly, but it adds boilerplate to your code.

Dependency Walker and dumpbin.exe (Windows)

On Windows Dependency Walker is a must-have for inspecting the dependencies of programs and libraries. http://dependencywalker.com/

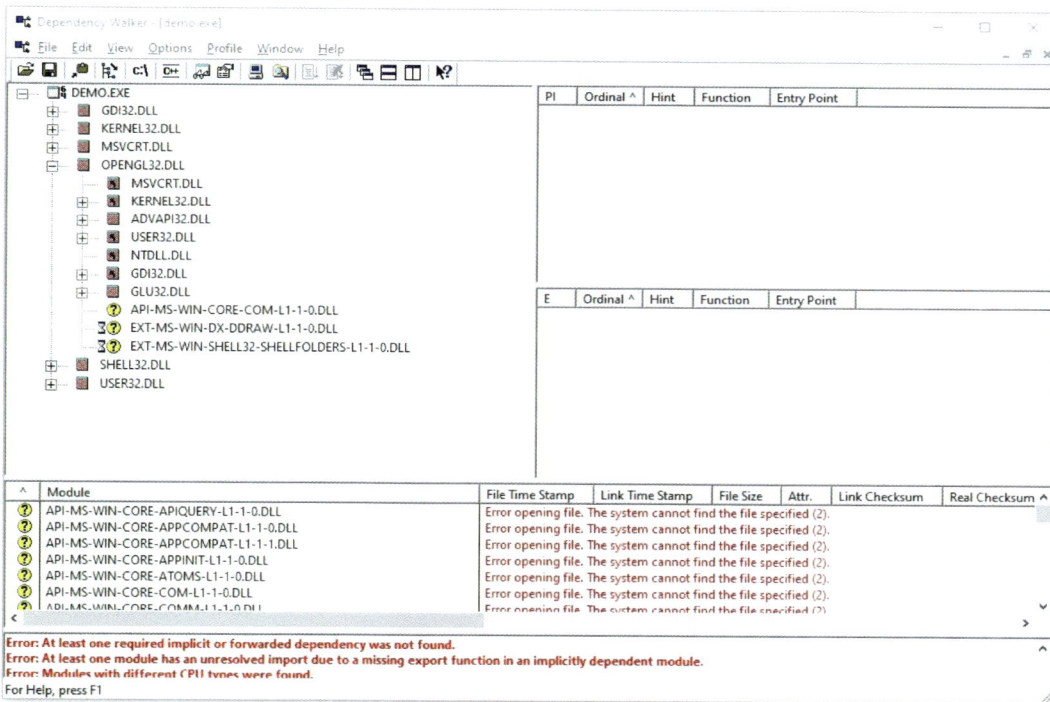

Figure 12.1. Dependency Walker gives you an interactive tree view of the external library dependencies for any program, and where they are being found on the system.

If you hit the 'view full paths' button you should also get a list of where your program is currently finding each library.

- You can ignore system files such as `kernel32.dll`, `user32.dll`, `gdi32.dll`, and `shell32.dll` - these are core to Windows.
- You can ignore any graphics drivers, and `OpenGL32.dll`, which will install with a user's video driver updates.
- `msvcrt.dll` is the C Run Time. For Visual Studio you will see e.g. `vcruntime140.dll`, and we need to think about bundling that somehow.

If you are using Visual Studio there is also a program called `dumpbin` that you can call from within Visual Studio's Developer Command Prompt tool. It will list a program or library's dependencies when you use the `/DEPENDENTS` flag.

Your program might run using the `msvcrt.dll` that comes with a user's Windows install. If you have compiled with MinGW GCC this is the one being used, and you don't need to do anything. Microsoft, however, recommends not relying on this, as there is no guarantee of stability between versions of the library.

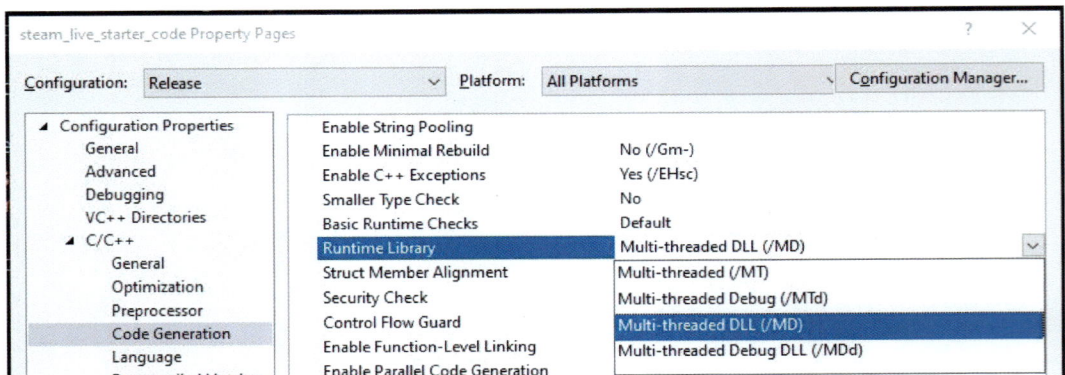

Figure 12.2. Visual Studio will static compile the CRT when the Runtime Library option is /MT.

For Visual Studio builds, where you will see a version number in the CRT filename, you can:

- Have the user install the Visual C++ redistributable package that matches your compiler. You can find these on the Microsoft website.
- Statically compile the runtime into your app. This is a good idea! Find the *Runtime Library* option in your project's *Property Pages* under *C/C++*, and switch it from /MD to /MT.

- Drop the required DLL files into the same folder as your .exe, and bundle that together for distribution. See https://docs.microsoft.com/en-us/visualstudio/releases/2019/redistribution

If you run Dependency Walker or `dumpbin` again on your binary after static compilation of dependencies you should see a much smaller list.

```
C:\WINDOWS\system32\cmd.exe

C:\Users\anton\projects\Project1\x64\Release>dumpbin /DEPENDENTS Project1.exe
Microsoft (R) COFF/PE Dumper Version 14.22.27905.0
Copyright (C) Microsoft Corporation.  All rights reserved.


Dump of file Project1.exe

File Type: EXECUTABLE IMAGE

  Image has the following dependencies:

    KERNEL32.dll

  Summary

        2000 .data
        1000 .pdata
        A000 .rdata
        1000 .reloc
        1000 .rsrc
       11000 .text
        1000 _RDATA

C:\Users\anton\projects\Project1\x64\Release>
```

Figure 12.3. Dumpbin reports `Project1.exe` only depends on `kernel32.dll`. Success!

ldd (Linux)

To get a list of all of the dependencies of your binary, and their dependencies, you can run `ldd`. It's more helpful to split the output by direct dependencies, and dependencies of dependencies. You can also find this information, and more details, with `readelf` or `objdump`.

```
ldd -v ./my_program
readelf -d ./my_program
objdump -x ./my_program
```

You will find the direct dependencies of your program under the first sections of each command's output.

Figure 12.4. `ldd` reports that my program directly depends on a local library (that it can't find) called `libsecond.so`.

To have your binary look for shared object libraries in a local subdirectory, rather than a system directory, you can:

1. Create a build script that sets the LD_RUN_PATH environment variable before compiling.

```
#!/bin/bash
export LD_RUN_PATH=\$ORIGIN/my_libs/
gcc -o my_program main.c -lmylib -Lmy_libs/
```

The \$ORIGIN part means *"relative to the location of the binary"*. Otherwise it will look for `my_libs/` relative to your current working directory, which isn't as useful.

2. Or create a run script that users will run instead of your binary. This will

119

set LD_LIBRARY_PATH.

```
#!/bin/bash
export LD_LIBRARY_PATH=\$ORIGIN/my_libs/
./my_program
```

3. Or set the -rpath flag to the linker, ld, with the relative path to your libraries. If you are not invoking the linker directly, you can send linker commands through GCC with -Wl.

```
gcc -o my_program main.c -lmylib -Lmy_libs/ -Wl,-rpath,\$ORIGIN/my_libs/
```

The relative path to your library comes after -rpath, following the comma.

```
anton:~/projects/howto_guides_pvt/book_testing/06_dynamic_lib[master]$ ldd my_program
        linux-vdso.so.1 (0x00007ffc86cb0000)
        libsecond.so => /home/anton/projects/howto_guides_pvt/book_testing/06_dynamic_
lib/./lib/libsecond.so (0x00007fee08ba0000)
        libc.so.6 => /lib/x86_64-linux-gnu/libc.so.6 (0x00007fee087af000)
        /lib64/ld-linux-x86-64.so.2 (0x00007fee08fa4000)
```

Figure 12.5. After building in the library path ldd now shows the program finds libsecond.so in a local directory.

4. Have your program open the library in code using dlopen(), then look for functions and hook them up to function pointers using dlsym().

With one of these methods you should then be able to create an archive of your binary, your assets folder, and your lib/ folder, and distribute it.

otool and `install_name_tool` (macOS)

Similar to `ldd`, on macOS we can use `otool` to find the shared objects a binary will try to link to:

```
otool -L ./my_program
```

MacOS shared object libraries have the `.dylib` extension, but you will also see framework files such as `Cocoa.framework`. These are a bundle comprising dylibs and header files for development. You don't need to redistribute system frameworks.

If you want to bundle a library with your program then you may need to change where your program looks for the library. It might run now, but if you send it to a friend it might not run on their computer, even if you copy the library file with it. They may also want to run your program from another working directory. The best solution is to make sure your program looks for the library in a path relative to itself. To change the path to a library for a binary we can use `install_name_tool`.

```
install_name_tool -change /old/path/libmylibrary.dylib \
@executable_path/libs/libmylibrary.dylib ./my_program
```

The `-change` command modifies our binary so that it looks for the library in the directory we prefer.

1. The first argument is the application's previous path to the library. Get this from `otool -L`.
2. The second argument is the new path. The `@executable_path` variable makes this relative to the directory of the binary, rather than relative to the user's current working directory.
3. The third argument is the filename of the binary to modify.

Run `otool -L` again on your binary to see changes.

If you move a library into a local folder you can use `otool -D ./mylib.dylib` to check its internal ID. This should also be a path relative to the executable that links against it. You can change the ID with `install_name_tool -id`.

```
install_name_tool -id @executable_path/libs/libmylibrary.dylib \
libs/libmylibrary.dylib
```

1. The first argument is the path to the library, relative to the program.
2. The second argument is the library file to modify.

These two commands should allow you to bundle your library in a directory with the binary and run your program from another working directory. See the man page for `install_name_tool` for more options.

App Bundles

MacOS and iOS applications are commonly redistributed in an application bundle. This is just a directory with a standardised structure, and the `.app` filename extension. All of the assets, the binary, and your bundled `.dylib` shared objects sit within the bundle, but it appears to be a single executable program to the user. You can have Xcode create the app bundle for you, or you can manually create it. There is sufficient documentation for creating the structure on the Apple website under Bundle Structures on developer.apple.com.

If you create your own bundle, you will need to use `install_name_tool`, as in the previous section because it will always be launched from an external working directory. You can write a script to create the bundle, copy files into the directory structure, and invoke `install_name_tool` on the program binary and any libraries as part of your build process.

App Containers and Package Managers

Although not specific to C, it's possible to avoid dependency bundling issues almost entirely - for non-graphical programs - by using a **container** or **sandbox** technology. These solutions add another layer of software (and installation) to insulate your program from the actual operating system with all the bits it needs to run. Docker https://www.docker.com/ is very popular, particularly for distributing otherwise messy systems of several programs and libraries that need to work together.

To share programs across Linux distributions the package management systems Flatpak https://flatpak.org/ and Snappy https://snapcraft.io/ provide solutions for building your program once for Linux, and reliably sharing it that it will run with all the correct libraries on most distributions of Linux.

Taking on any additional software layers has a complexity and reliability cost too that must be accounted for. It's always worth reducing the complexity of your software and build. Ideally you can distribute it without needing additional packaging software.

Tips and Common Problems

- Microsoft provides guide documentation on distributing and packaging programs built with Visual Studio
  https://docs.microsoft.com/en-us/cpp/windows/determining-which-dlls-to-redistribute
- Daniel Gibson has a good blog article about shipping binaries for Linux *How to create portable Linux binaries, Nov. 2017.*
  https://blog.gibson.sh/2017/11/26/creating-portable-linux-binaries/
- Do not distribute libraries with your software that you have not licenced! Some of this software is charged **per programmer per month** - be extremely careful or you could face a huge bill and legal problems. I've caught this happening in commercial software!
- Maintain and update an inventory of all of your dependencies' licences to prevent breaches. The licences of dependencies and your project's need for them can change, so reserve time to audit libraries between major releases.
- When distributing shared/dynamic libraries with your binary make sure you have the files with the same architecture as your program's build.
- You may not be permitted to distribute debug versions of core programming libraries.
- Debug builds of libraries often have a *d* at the end of their filename.
- You may not be permitted to static compile some libraries into your software.
- Don't static compile commonly-used utility libraries that get frequent updates and security patches. Allow the user to replace the shared libraries with newer versions to patch vulnerabilities. They can't do that if the libraries are static compiled into your program - you'd need to ship a new binary. This exception includes any library that accesses the Internet, and any libraries that interact with device drivers and operating system specific functionality.

- C++ libraries have various language features that cause the ABI to be less stable between library versions, and incompatible between compilers. If you need to use or make a library, a preference for C over C++ libraries can avoid a lot of these frustrating problems that can stop your program running. You can write a C interface for a C++ library, which may help.
- Make sure you test your program on machines that never had any developer tools installed - your program may be dynamically linking to system-installed libraries that other users won't have. A fresh system install per release test, e.g. on a new virtual machine, can spot missing dependencies.
- On Visual Studio your default folder structure and binary output location probably don't match how you want your final program's folder structure to look. Asset locations may be in a different relative directory. Under project settings you can configure the project's binary output locations to be in a sensible place so that the relative path to your assets makes more sense.
- Consider giving your debug and release binaries different file names so you don't mix them up during testing or bundling.
- Remove unstable compiler flags that may have crept in like `-ffast-math`, or `-Ofast`, and enable disabled warnings.
- Compile on different compilers to collect any missed warnings.
- Compile your release build with optimisation flags to improve performance of C++ templates etc.
- Run static analysis tools, sanitisers, and memory leak checkers.
- Before distributing, leave your program running overnight, or for a few days, to pop out any bugs with memory leaks, floating point error accumulations, or overflowing timers.
- Have someone that wasn't involved in the development process go through the install and testing process - it's usually much more fiddly and error-prone than developers are aware of.
- Try testing your bundled application on as many real machines and hardware configurations as possible - virtual machines will hide real hardware issues. A common hardware support issue these days is high-DPI monitors. Does your app run properly at 1440p and above on different monitors?
- Invest time to create a one-command (or one click) build, test & bundle script that does your entire app compile, version number stamp, any

smoke tests, and bundles for a release. A multi-step or fiddly process will cause avoidable problems and delays.

- Have a QA (quality assurance) testing process and sign-off step after every release is built, and before it gets published. If a team is putting everything together the rush or the clash of different completed systems, tested against earlier versions of the codebase, can create lots of issues that need to be caught.
- Create a Release Notes document with new features and known issues, which can help manage expectations of users and reduce duplicate bug reports.
- On GNU/Linux you can get away with asking the user to have a few basic shared libraries, and some Linux users prefer this as part of the philosophy over statically compiled libraries. They'd like it even more if you distributed your program as source code, which is sometimes viable even for commercial software.
- Creating a distribution-specific package, like a `.deb` for Ubuntu and Debian with a tool like `dpkg-buildpackage` is the most 'native' sort of installer, but sometimes just distributing a `tar.gz` archive that extracts and runs from a user's local folder is fine.
- Have a system to capture user feedback and bug reports.
- Allow users to send you a log or a dump if the program crashes.
- Include user system specs in the reports you get to identify troublesome system configurations.

13 *Argh! My New Job is on Linux!* Unix Tools

Unix-derived operating systems were built with a philosophy of many mini-programs interacting with each other on the command line. You can get a lot of productive common tasks done by using little programs, rather than library functions in your own program. If I'm working on these systems I often have a terminal window open for quick tasks. Unix-derived systems include GNU/Linux, Solaris, Minix, and BSD-derivatives, such as FreeBSD and Apple's macOS.

Linux systems and command-line software is everywhere in tech that has anything to do with the web, servers, or micro-controllers. Everyone eventually needs to use Git on the command-line. It's quite common in the tech industry to jump to a new operating system between roles, and I'm also here thinking of that scenario.

"Argh! I'm on Linux in my new job, how do I work productively without a degree in Linux?".

I'm assuming, reading this, you're already familiar with the absolute basics `ls`, `cd`, `rm`, and `mkdir`, and how to use your distribution's **package manager** to install software from repositories. If you're coming from Windows and need a basic text editor on the command line, try `nano` - it has the key commands on-screen.

Windows Subsystem for Linux

It's possible to set up Microsoft's Windows Subsystem for Linux (WSL) on Windows 10. This can be a handy terminal to have open for quick programming manual page look-ups, and also lets you use Linux development tools like Valgrind, without requiring a full system installation or dual-booting. To try this out follow the instructions on the Microsoft website https://docs.microsoft.com/en-us/windows/wsl/install-win10 which will let you then install a Linux distribution such as Ubuntu or Debian through the Microsoft Store app.

Figure 13.1. Ubuntu running on Windows Subsystem for Linux. It's in a window on a Windows 10 desktop.

With your own Linux-in-a-window you can access the folders on your Windows computer under `/mnt/c/`. You can install tools and software through the distribution's package managers.

There are some small niggles between operating systems when processing files saved with MS-DOS carriage return \r at the end of lines, but you can change that by opening your file in nano `my_file.sh` and switching line-endings mode on save (CTRL+O then ALT+D).

- Be careful creating files in Windows directories. Windows is not case-sensitive, so avoid having two copies of a file where only the case differs, or one may not be accessible from Windows.
- Be careful creating directories in Windows directories with WSL - they will be flagged case-sensitive by default (at the time of writing this). Use `fsutil.exe` on Windows to check or modify this status.
- Keep an eye on updates - WSL is very new and integrations with tools and fixes for issues change frequently.
- You can also now run GNU/Linux commands like `bash ./my_script.sh` **from a Windows terminal,** which can be handy for small tasks.

RTFM with man

Unix systems use a system called **man pages** to store user manuals for programs, programming library functions, system calls, and other tools. If a command tool, such as GCC, has a manual installed

```
man gcc
```

This should give you a summary of the different command line flags or options, examples, and any caveats or warnings. Man pages are grouped into numbered sections.

- Section 1 - User commands.
- Section 2 - System calls.
- Section 3 - Library functions.
- ...

To quickly look up the documentation for a library function we can specify section 3, then the function name to look up its manual.

```
man 3 fprintf
```

Press *space* or *page down* to move down, q to quit, or /, followed by an expression or word, to search for that.

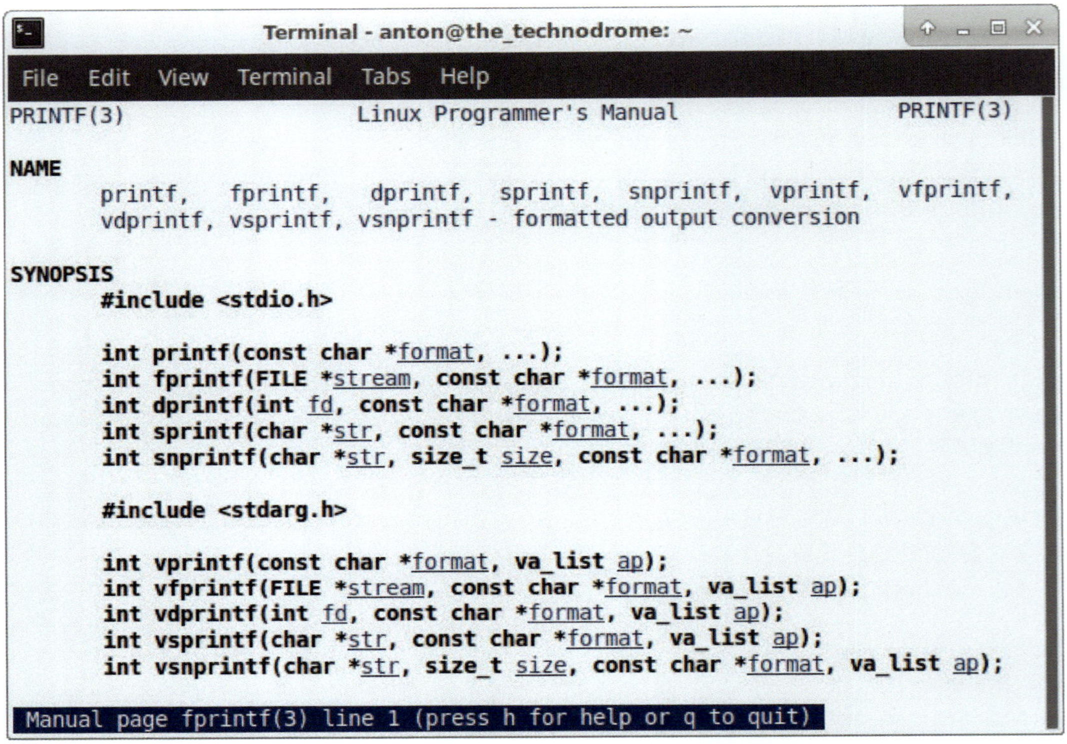

Figure 13.2. The man-pages for the `printf` family of functions.

I use this all the time when working on Linux or Mac - it's usually quicker than Googling. And usually far more correct than what you're likely to find on top-voted Stack Overflow responses to questions!

- Man pages should always be your **first** reference, Google for additional information - usually this is a caveat not considered in the man pages like *"This function is not portable to Windows, use XYZ instead."*

View Directory Structure with `tree`

The `ls` command is similar to `dir` on Windows. For a tree view of directories and their contents install and run `tree`.

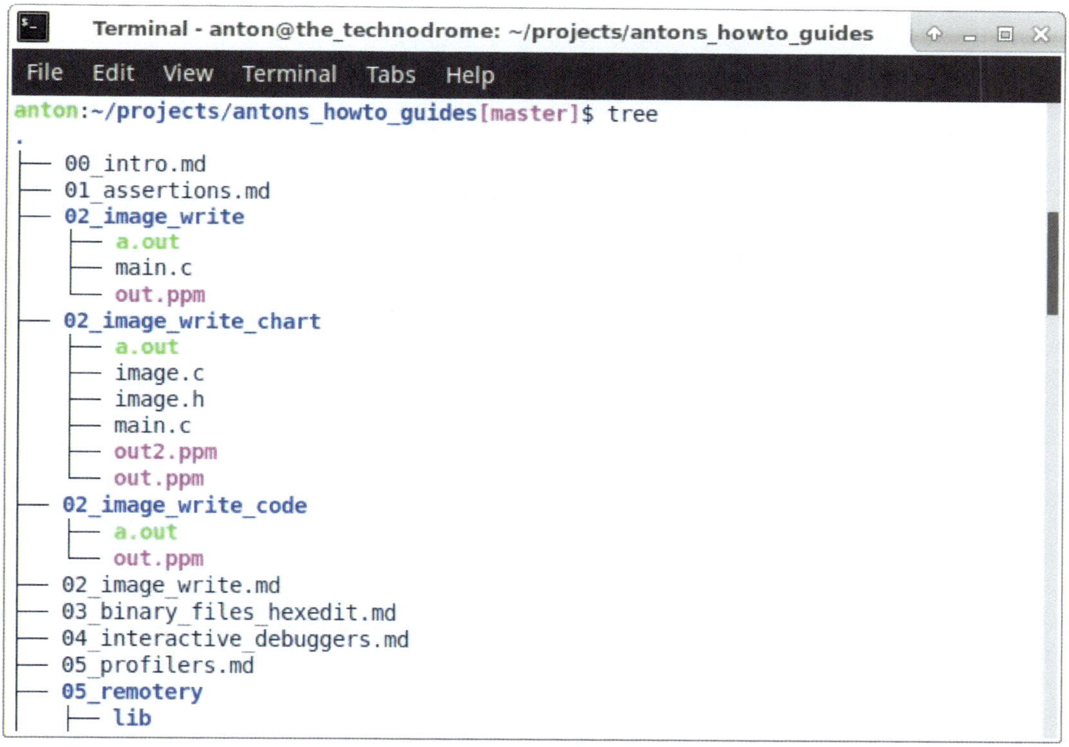

```
Terminal - anton@the_technodrome: ~/projects/antons_howto_guides

File    Edit    View    Terminal    Tabs    Help

anton:~/projects/antons_howto_guides[master]$ tree
.
├── 00_intro.md
├── 01_assertions.md
├── 02_image_write
│   ├── a.out
│   ├── main.c
│   └── out.ppm
├── 02_image_write_chart
│   ├── a.out
│   ├── image.c
│   ├── image.h
│   ├── main.c
│   ├── out2.ppm
│   └── out.ppm
├── 02_image_write_code
│   ├── a.out
│   └── out.ppm
├── 02_image_write.md
├── 03_binary_files_hexedit.md
├── 04_interactive_debuggers.md
├── 05_profilers.md
├── 05_remotery
│   ├── lib
```

Figure 13.3. A complete tree picture of project directory structure and contents.

Find in Files with grep

You can very quickly search through the contents of files for a particular keyword, sentence, or fragment, using `grep`. `man grep` for the full list of options. I use this when I want to quickly find any and every place in any file that calls a particular function, or uses a particular variable.

```
grep -irn "my_function_name" src/
```

- `-i` does a case-insensitive search for the term or expression given - `"my_function_name"`.
- `-r` searches recursively, in all files from the folder given - `src/`.
- `-n` prints the line number beside each match found.
- You can give a specific file, or a list of files, instead of a directory.

Search and Replace with sed

Sed is a match-and-replace program for streams. I most commonly use it as a *find-and-replace* across files, which can be handy for refactoring a function name, although risky.

```
sed -i 's/my_old_function_name/new_function_name/g' *.c
```

This will replace any match of `my_old_function_name` with `new_function_name` found in any `.c` files.

- *Caveat* - `sed` on Linux and macOS have slightly different interfaces, so scripts using `sed` aren't always portable between systems.
- If you have functions called `my_old_function_name_b` they will also become `new_function_name_b`. *Woops!*
- `-i` means "*modify the file **in place**". If you leave this out it will write to `stdout` instead, which you could use for double-checking changes.
- You can have `sed` write a backup of the original files if you supply an extension to use to `-i`, so `-i.bak`. On macOS the `-i` command always requires an extension.
- You can use `sed` in this way to fix common typos and spelling errors too.
- If the slash `/` is part of the expressions then you may use a different separator character.

```
sed -i 's#my_old_function_name#new_function_name#g' *.c
```

Count Lines of Code with wc and cloc

The wc (word count) command counts newlines, words, and bytes in a file, where the first value gives us a rough line count.

```
wc main.cpp
31 147 914 main.cpp
```

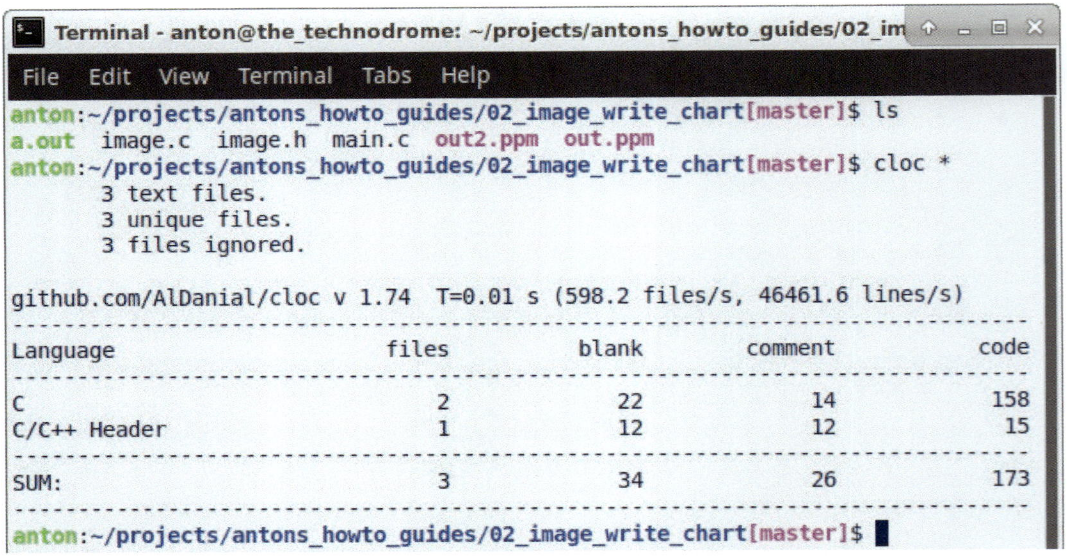

Figure 13.4. cloc *counts lines of code, excluding whitespace, and knows many languages.*

For a more accurate lines-of-code count, including comments, you can install a program called *cloc* https://github.com/AlDanial/cloc. This is available in Linux and HomeBrew repositories (for macOS), and can also be installed natively on Windows.

Redirect and Pipe `stdout`, `stderr`, or `stdin`

Each program has 3 standard input/output "streams":

- 0 - `stdin` - Standard input. Used for user-entered command-line text, reading output from other programs with `read()`.
- 1 - `stdout` - Standard output. Used by `printf()`. Typically buffered.
- 2 - `stderr` - Standard error. Used for error print-outs. Typically not buffered.

You will often see command-line scripts that chain the inputs and outputs of several programs together using pipe `|`, get-input-from-file `<`, redirect-output-to-file `>`, and append-to-file `>>`.

The most common use is to write the `stdout` of a program to a text file.

```
./my_program > stdout_file.txt
```

You can also write only the error output to a file by specifying file stream 2 for `stderr`.

```
./my_program 2> stderr_file.txt
```

Pipe `|` connects the `stdout` of a program to the stdin of another program. You can, for example, search for a word in the output of a program

```
cat test_data.txt | grep "Hello"
```

To redirect a program's `stdin` from a file you can use `<`.

```
./my_program < test_data.txt
```

- You can chain several programs' inputs and outputs together in this way,

in one command.
- These mostly work the same on Windows too, although in PowerShell you cannot use the < operator.
- To reduce output of a command (or program) to just the top or bottom few lines, you can pipe the result to head or tail, respectively, and then again redirect that to a file if you wish.

```
ps aux | tail > shorter_output.txt
```

- tail can also be handy for dealing with big system log files, where you only care about the last hour or so.

Concatenate Files with `cat`

The `cat` command, given one file as an argument, will print its contents to `stdout`. Given more than one file, it concatenates their contents one-after-the-other.

```
cat first.c second.c > combined.c
```

This creates a file combining the contents of the first two files. You could also append to a file by using the `>>` operator instead of `>`.

List Process IDs with `ps`

`ps` reports a snapshot of currently-running processes on the system. Windows PowerShell has a `ps` command, and there is also a `tasklist` command on Windows to do similar.

By default `ps` only lists your own user-owned processes. The most commonly used invocation of `ps` is `ps aux`, which shows (**a**)ll processes, and their (**u**)ser or owner, and (**x**) processes not attached to a user or terminal.

Monitor Resource Usage with `top` and `htop`

```
 ┌──────────────────────────────────────────────────────────────────────┐
 │ ▛     Terminal - anton@the_technodrome: ~            ⬆ _ ▢ X │
 ├──────────────────────────────────────────────────────────────────────┤
 │  File  Edit  View  Terminal  Tabs  Help                                │
 │ top - 16:36:24 up 59 min,  1 user,  load average: 0.96, 1.03, 1.13     │
 │ Tasks: 257 total,   2 running, 182 sleeping,   0 stopped,   1 zombie   │
 │ %Cpu(s):  7.4 us,  2.5 sy,  0.0 ni, 89.9 id,  0.2 wa,  0.0 hi,  0.0 si,  0.0 st │
 │ KiB Mem : 32863552 total, 23678392 free,  3515468 used,  5669692 buff/cache │
 │ KiB Swap: 16698876 total, 16698876 free,        0 used. 28404480 avail Mem │
 │                                                                        │
 │   PID USER      PR  NI    VIRT    RES    SHR S  %CPU %MEM     TIME+ COMMAND │
 │ 14321 anton     20   0 3097612 428092 186272 S  19.3  1.3  5:17.98 Web Content │
 │ 10002 anton     20   0 3582356 948144 232660 S  14.3  2.9  8:09.45 Web Content │
 │  9228 anton     20   0  443932  36648  26768 S  11.3  0.1  0:00.95 panel-1-wh+ │
 │  9934 anton     20   0 3982736 610908 346620 S  10.6  1.9  8:16.73 firefox │
 │  1268 root      20   0  467584 134048  88808 S  10.3  0.4  5:04.58 Xorg │
 │ 10130 anton     20   0 3372472 544712 145500 S   4.3  1.7  3:51.13 Web Content │
 │  9101 anton     20   0  716712  76828  38252 S   3.7  0.2  0:04.40 xfdesktop │
 │  9199 anton      9 -11 1385440  17800  13580 R   3.0  0.1  0:42.47 pulseaudio │
 │ 16633 anton     20   0  532320  37036  27408 S   3.0  0.1  0:00.71 xfce4-term+ │
 │ 16850 anton     20   0  372736  26912  21500 S   2.0  0.1  0:00.06 xfce4-scre+ │
 │  9093 anton     20   0  189224  24892  20028 S   0.7  0.1  0:05.05 xfwm4 │
 │  9253 anton     20   0  346184  27960  21288 S   0.7  0.1  0:24.48 panel-14-s+ │
 │ 16848 anton     20   0   41908   3780   3064 R   0.7  0.0  0:00.15 top │
 │  1289 root     -51   0       0      0      0 S   0.3  0.0  0:05.08 irq/148-nv+ │
 │  8983 anton     20   0   50724   5244   3852 S   0.3  0.0  0:00.89 dbus-daemon │
 │  9380 anton     20   0 1136544 212744  80088 S   0.3  0.6  0:14.93 Discord │
 │ 10058 anton     20   0 20.677g 306964 110576 S   0.3  0.9  1:25.32 WebExtensi+ │
 └──────────────────────────────────────────────────────────────────────┘
```

Figure 13.5. The `top` *program is an interactive process monitor.*

`top` is a process monitor. You can watch your program's resource consumption, or find out if your program is running slowly because something else is using all the resources. The hungriest processes are at the top of the list, where you can also see its process identifier (PID), with percentages of CPU and memory consumed.

- Get a list of interactive commands with the ? key.
- Spacebar immediately refreshes the list. Change the update interval with s.
- If you run `top` as a super user (e.g. `sudo top`) then a process can be *re-niced* with r to increase or reduce its priority on the system. Lower

"nice" numbers have higher priority.
- You can kill a process with k.

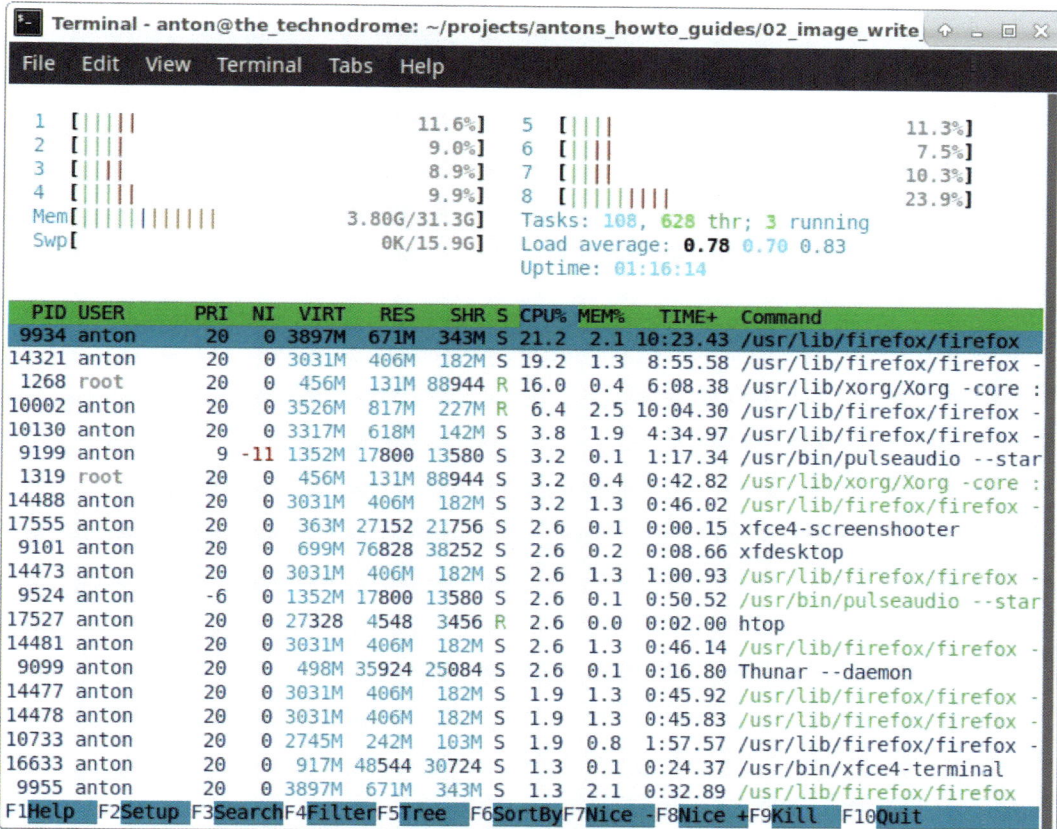

Figure 13.6. The htop process monitor provides visualisations and different view filters.

A more sophisticated version called htop can be installed. It's a bit easier to read, and has visualisations of a sort, to give a clearer picture of overall system CPU core utilisation and memory consumption.

Force Quit a Process with `kill`, `killall`, and `xkill`

The `kill` command sends a signal to a process with a given PID (which you can get from `ps` or `top`).

- By default it sends `SIGTERM` signal, which terminates processes that don't intercept that signal.
- This often doesn't work, so you can `kill -9` to send the signal 9, `SIGKILL`, which can not be caught.
- For a list of signals `man 7 signal`. They differ slightly between operating systems.
- `killall` kills processes by name, rather than PID.
- `xkill` is a program you may be able to install on X-based desktops. It turns your mouse cursor into a skull in some versions, and you can kill unresponsive apps by clicking on their window.

Timing a Program with `time` and `/usr/bin/time`

To time a program or command you can use the `time` command, or the more detailed `/usr/bin/time`.

```
time ./my_program
/usr/bin/time ./my_program
```

The basic results give
- *real time* or *wall clock time* - how long it took if you timed it using a real wrist watch, or a clock on your wall.
- *user time* - how long your program's functions spent running.
- *system time* - how long your program's system calls, such as file I/O, took.

The `/usr/bin/time` program can give additional statistics in verbose mode -v.

```
anton:~/projects/howto_guides_pvt/book_testing/02_image_write_chart[master]$
time ./my_program

real    0m0.005s
user    0m0.005s
sys     0m0.000s
anton:~/projects/howto_guides_pvt/book_testing/02_image_write_chart[master]$
/usr/bin/time -v ./my_program
        Command being timed: "./my_program"
        User time (seconds): 0.01
        System time (seconds): 0.00
        Percent of CPU this job got: 92%
        Elapsed (wall clock) time (h:mm:ss or m:ss): 0:00.01
        Average shared text size (kbytes): 0
        Average unshared data size (kbytes): 0
        Average stack size (kbytes): 0
        Average total size (kbytes): 0
        Maximum resident set size (kbytes): 1728
        Average resident set size (kbytes): 0
        Major (requiring I/O) page faults: 0
        Minor (reclaiming a frame) page faults: 111
        Voluntary context switches: 1
        Involuntary context switches: 0
        Swaps: 0
        File system inputs: 0
        File system outputs: 400
        Socket messages sent: 0
        Socket messages received: 0
        Signals delivered: 0
        Page size (bytes): 4096
        Exit status: 0
anton:~/projects/howto_guides_pvt/book_testing/02_image_write_chart[master]$
```

Figure 13.7. Two different timers collecting user, system, and real run time for a program called `my_program`.

It is also possible to collect the running time and other statistics using the `perf` profiler on Linux:

```
sudo perf stat ./my_program
```

Closing Remarks

We hope this book introduced you to some useful tools for improving your work, and that you enjoyed the presentation. We intend to expand the availability of this work in other formats and to other distributors. If you have any preferences in this regard please let us know.

We would love to produce further resources, and do lots more illustrations and cartoons to help with other subjects. Look out for future volumes! If you think this style would work well with another topic please also send a request.

Dr Anton Gerdelan and Dr Katja Žibrek

Acknowledgements

Special thanks to Clare Conran and the excellent people at the ADAPT Centre for hosting at Trinity College Dublin and encouraging the start of this work.

We would like to thank the following reviewers for their invaluable insights and corrections:

Timothy Costigan	Francisco Lopez Luro	Darren Sweeney
Margaret Greer	Andrew Moss	Kim Restad
Hugh Fitzpatrick	Daniel Playne	Andre Weissflog
Sergey Kosarevsky	Saija Sorsa	

Thanks to Daniel Gibson for comments and suggestions on assertions that are incorporated here. Thanks to Don Williamson for advice about, and images, of Remotery. Thanks again to Saija Sorsa for training me in the art of fuzzing software. Thanks to Rowan Hughes for advice. Thanks to Rich Geldreich for encouraging the use of fuzzers, which set this work in a good direction. Thanks to Claire Cunningham for design advice.

About the Authors

Anton Gerdelan

I am a computer graphics programmer, living in Ireland. I earned a PhD in Computer Science from Massey University in New Zealand. I wrote a graphics book called *Anton's OpenGL 4 Tutorials*, which surprised me when it immediately became very popular. I worked for an Augmented Reality headset company called Daqri, which involved working with a lot of different engineers in offices around the world, and coordinating our work remotely for some pretty fantastic technology. I've done quite a bit of lecturing at universities, and make video games as a hobby.

Katja Žibrek

I am a researcher in graphics, currently residing in France and working at the Inria research institute. I studied Psychology at the University of Ljubljana, Slovenia, where I got introduced to Virtual Reality as a potential tool to study people. I needed to know more about graphics, so I continued with a PhD in Computer Science at Trinity College Dublin, Ireland. Because of my suspicious social science background it is probably better I stayed away from writing any parts of the book but I made some pretty pictures.

Printed in Poland
by Amazon Fulfillment
Poland Sp. z o.o., Wrocław